A GOLDEN TREASURY OF CHINESE POETRY

This book is published
with the aid of
a grant from
THE ASIA FOUNDATION

RENDITIONS Books
are issued by the Centre for Translation
Projects, The Chinese University of Hong
Kong, publisher of *Renditions*, a Chinese-
English Translation Magazine.

A Golden Treasury of Chinese Poetry

121 Classical Poems

Translated by
John A. Turner, S.J.

with Notes and Chinese Texts

Compiled and Edited
by
John J. Deeney

With the Assistance of
Kenneth K. B. Li

A *RENDITIONS* Book

The Chinese University of Hong Kong
Distributed by the University of Washington Press
Seattle and London

First published 1976 by
The Centre for Translation Projects
The Chinese University of Hong Kong

Library of Congress Catalog Card Number 75-42790

11-29-76

ISBN 0-295-955-06-6

Printed by
SING TAO NEWSPAPERS LTD.
Offset Printing Department
Hong Kong

Contents

Preface

THE MERIT of this particular collection is that the translations themselves are poetry and that almost the entire range and variety of Chinese poetry is covered through the sensitive rendering and learned sensibility of a single translator. My editorial policy has been to let Father Turner speak for himself. Consequently, the translations themselves have not been tampered with in the least and the editions of the Chinese originals which he used have been followed. The notes to the translations at the back of the book are mostly Father Turner's, additional material being supplied only when felt to be useful or essential for a better understanding and appreciation of the poem. The notes include background materials, biographical sketches, literal translations, notable divergencies from the common interpretation, etc.

The posthumous Introduction is virtually pure Turner (taken from his correspondence and unpublished essays), the editor merely supplying transitional phrases between his fragmentary observations and emending only when this was absolutely necessary for clarity. Obvious typographical errors have been silently corrected. This Introduction is an integral part of the anthology since it elucidates Father Turner's translation policy and, although fragmentary, provides a consistent and fairly comprehensive view of the problems of translation in the context of Chinese literature.

The unexpectedness of Father Turner's death made the task of gathering together the manuscripts a very difficult one. When first entering his room, I had something of the feeling of awe and despair that must have accompanied the first scholars who

1

penetrated the Qumran caves in search of the Dead Sea Scrolls. But once all the materials had been sorted out, the pieces of the puzzle (even the damaged or incomplete ones) began to fit together. My personal acquaintance with the author and interviews with his intimate friends and admirers helped to reduce guess-work to a minimum.

Most Chinese poets give no titles to their poems. In this anthology, I have accepted the attribution of titles invented by the translator (prefixed to poems that have either no title at all or else an ambiguous one or one which might be puzzling to a non-Chinese reader) and retained the quotation marks which he used to designate poetic genres and original titles which were mysterious or problematic. Generally speaking, the poems have been arranged in a chronological order and the Wade-Giles system of romanization used.

The selection of poems necessarily depends on the personal preferences (and prejudices) of the translator and the editor. In this collection, over 75 poets are represented. Father Turner's intentions were clear from the more than 300 poems he laboured over for almost 35 years. Almost every major poetic genre is represented. On the other hand, his independence of judgment was shown in his attitude toward Chinese poets of great critical reputation. He had the deepest respect for Tu Fu and Su Tung-p'o but, rather surprisingly, did not care for the work of T'ao Yüan-ming at all. In reference to his version of T'ao's famous poem, "Peach-Blossom Fount" (p. 77), he says quite candidly:

> I deliberately chose this longish poem because
> I dislike T'ao Yüan-ming and his poetry intense-
> ly, but, since he is an eminent figure, I wished
> to be over and done with him: that is why I
> subconsciously used a metre like Dryden's,
> whose poetry, I am regretful to admit, I do not
> like.

2

Some of the major themes of the poems he selected are: Nature-Pastoral (30 poems), Separation-Loneliness (29), Transience-Death (22), Love-Friendship (17), Social Criticism (9) and Melancholy (9). In a letter to a friend Father Turner had to admit: "I have too many poems that are sad and serious, and am trying to add in some odd and funny ones." In the final stages of his selection policy, he wrote: "Most of the poems I have done are *popular* ones (which again will be of advantage to the *learner* of Chinese): indeed a point of selection which guided me somewhat in the earlier pieces is their containing of a phrase which has become proverbial. The rest I choose for their charm and translatableness combined. A few I have chosen because of their difficulty."

From an editorial point of view, my selection of the 121 poems out of our 300 was based on: fidelity to the original, brilliancy of execution and fresh representation of the tradition. Father Turner felt that he could often preserve the succinctness and come near to the form of the original Chinese in an English translation. When a famous critic asserted that the lines

萬壑樹聲滿
千崖秋風高

could never be translated into a corresponding ten syllables of English verse, Father Turner wrote his reaction in a letter to a friend:

> Immediately on reading this article, at a library table, I wrote in the margin of the paper, in the presence of friends who may or may not remember so slight a bit of versifying:
>
> Vales of rustling trees,
> Cliffs where winds blow high

There is no necessity to translate "autumn", for autumn is the season of high winds. And myriad and thousand is but a vasty poetic sign of plurality. The real difficulty is that the five-syllabled line, which is exceedingly difficult to manipulate in English, may sound hieratic like the pentasyllabics of Campbell, and so be un-suited to the tenor of the poem, whatever that may be.

Father Turner prided himself on the fact that his translations were, "in general, 'lean' and vigorous: some of them are emphatic". He vehemently denied that he "padded" his translations, since this would automatically "kill the vigour of a poem and enervate it". Rather, he referred to the fact that he usually translated "neat" and, in fact, often omitted. What seemed to be "padding" was, in fact, "artistic expansion", which he justified in the interests of greater perspicuity.

Sometimes a line must be omitted or expanded for the sake of clarity since the whole back-ground of English civilization is teetotally different from that of Chinese. The lengthening in Wang Wei's "Green Brook" (p. 103) is not an unwarranted expansion: it is a periphrasis to avoid bathos.

Blue water-bloom and river-bud
Wide are hurried adown the flood:
And reeds and bulrushes appear
In limpid waters mirrored clear.

漾漾汎菱荇
澄澄映葭葦

I am translating poetry. For "(a sort of) duck-weed" and "water-nut" I have substituted "Blue water-bloom and river-bud". The Chinese for "duckweed" is melodious and far from vulgar association. Shelley has used the same periphrasis for "duckweed" when he speaks of "starry river buds"—and he was writing straight English! So too for "water-nut" which has an exquisite pale-blue flower, a favourite of the Chinese. They often use it as an epithet for ladies' mirrors, in which case I would translate it "hyaline", meaning "watery-purplish-blue".

The four-line Chinese Epigram *chüeh chü* (絕句), is another case in point. It is so concentrated and tightly organized that it can hardly be reproduced in four lines of equivalent English. Father Turner's translations usually expand this type of verse into six or eight lines which are still brief enough to show their authenticity. For instance, take Chu Shu-chên's "Fallen Blossoms":

> Just as their buds were clustering
> Upon a twining spray,
> An envious storm came blustering
> And swept them all away.
> I'd like to tell the Lord of Spring
> He should assert his power,
> Nor have them on green moss to cling,
> Poor little flower on flower!

> 連理枝頭花正開，
> 妒花風雨便相催。
> 願教青帝常爲主，
> 莫遣紛紛點翠苔！

5

In attempting to recapture the flavour and style of the original, Father Turner chose to use traditional forms of English verse. When criticized about the "Victorian" tone of his translations, he defended himself by saying: "My style in verse-making is not 19th century: it is mainly pre-Miltonic *plus* 20th century, being conditioned by Chinese rhetoric. Certainly it would not easily appeal to enthusiasts for what is called Modern Poetry and to those who write about it." In his relatively rare moments of modesty, he would say that he was "often not sure about a poem until I had tried it out on somebody", but whatever his listener's opinion, he could never be deterred from translating into formal verse patterns. He would insist no one could be really faithful to the strict formalism of most Chinese verse and do anything but attempt a counterpart in English verse. What amazes the reader of his translations is his versatility in handling a wide variety of verse forms and his artistic use of rhyme.

Sometimes he strictly adheres to a traditional verse form such as the sonnet; for instance, his translation of Li Po's "Down from the Mountain" (see p. 109) is a perfect Shakespearean sonnet. On this poem he commented: "So fine and close-knit is Chinese poetic composition that a 14-line poem, with something of a 'kick' in the last two lines, almost inevitably resolves itself in translation into a sonnet". Similarly, in his translation of "Disappointment" (p. 41), we find a very concise equivalent of the original (exactly 48 English syllables [40 words] to 48 Chinese characters), where the metre and rhyme approximate to the original.

On other occasions he will use a very unusual verse structure, employing a wide variety of line lengths and rhyme schemes (see p. 92-3, and p. 244-5). He is also very adept at substituting a literary device common in English for another device in Chinese; for instance, the frequent repetition of words in the original "Wedding Song" (see p. 36) is virtually impossible to carry over into English, and so Father Turner makes up for it by a regular use of rhyme (not present in the original). One of the rare exceptions where rhyme is not employed is his translation of Yen Shu's "Mutability" (see p. 225).

Perhaps most outstanding of all is his ability to sustain long, narrative poems such as T'ao Yüan-ming's "Peach-Blossom Fount" in heroic couplets (p. 73) and Po Chü-i's "The Song of Enduring Woe" written predominantly in blank verse (p. 169). In reading his translation of Chang Chiu-ling's "The Waterfall" (p. 89) and comparing it with the original, one might get the impression that he was carried away by his own rhetoric. But a closer reading reveals that, for him, the meaning of the Chinese, like Shakespeare's language, largely depends upon rhythm. Consequently, a literal faithfulness gives way, in this *tour de force*, to a greater fidelity to the rhythm, which he insisted was of the essence of poetry.

This same "greater fidelity" to the demands of poetic translation directed Father Turner's artistic talents to the end of his life. His extraordinary versatility enabled him to produce the genuine poetry of remarkable quality which graces these pages.

John J. Deeney, S. J.

Acknowledgements

It was a pleasure to discover, among Fr. Turner's colleagues and friends, so many hands willing to help prepare this collection for publication as a tribute to the man they held in such esteem.

His fellow-Jesuits in Hong Kong (Fathers Fergus Cronin, John Russell, Matthew Corbally, Ciaran Kane, Carlo Kwan Wing-chung, Robert Ng Chi-fun) were always ready to extend a helpful hand when needed. A special debt of gratitude is due to Fr. Joseph Shields for preparing the manuscript and to Fr. Alan Birmingham for sharing (in interviews and in writing) his personal reminiscences.

Dr. Kenneth K.B. Li, a devoted friend of Fr. Turner's, a man of great poetic sensibility and the most conscientious collaborator I have ever worked with, deserves the largest share of praise. It was he who worked closest with the Chinese materials, supplementing biographical information, ferreting out the original poems, helping to select, date and order them.

My thanks are also due to my many scholar-friends in Taiwan for their critical reading of the poems, and to Mrs. Yeung Siu Lai-kin, Miss Rosemarie Braun and Miss Ch'en Hui-chu for their painstaking transcriptions from very difficult manuscript materials.

Finally, for seeing the manuscript through the final stages of the press, I am deeply grateful to the entire staff of the Chinese University of Hong Kong's Centre for Translation Projects, particularly to Miss Diana Yu, Managing Editor of the magazine *Renditions*, and Mrs. Fanny Chiu, who proofread the entire book with meticulous care. It was a pleasure to work with such a friendly group and a privilege to be chosen as the first title of *RENDITIONS* Books' distinguished series.   J.J.D.

Introduction*

The poems in this book are a selection of verse translations done by the author since he commenced the study of Chinese in 1935. Being as close to the originals as perspicuity, the requirements of English idiom and convention, and the author's limitations would permit, they may serve as well for the use of beginners in Chinese and students of Chinese poetry as for the interest or amusement of readers of English verse. They are entirely independent in style and syntax, and almost entirely in interpretation, of the work of previous translators into English.

My sole qualifications for attempting the work are a fair knowledge of the English and Chinese tongues, a certain familiarity with Chinese ways, an unbounded admiration of Chinese poetry, a fondness for versifying, and—the only criterion of true translation which encourages me to publish them—that my Chinese friends like them, and take them as authentic.

The translator's aim has been to make close translations of representative and popular Chinese poems, which should reproduce their style and spirit, and thus bring to readers of English a glimpse of the beauty which I see in Chinese poetry—the traditional poetry of Old China.

I say "Old China" because this to me means "beauty and order". Also because I want to show tacitly that the tradition of classical Chinese beauty is continuous and alive; and because I

---

*This Introduction is compiled from the writings of the late John Turner. Page references are given for poems cited to illustrate his translation methods. He also quoted or referred to other translations that are not included in the present volume.

personally loathe what is called "Modern China", the vulgarity, insincerity and imitativeness (of all that is shoddy in the West) that sprang from the 1919 May 4th Movement.

Chinese Literature is the high artistic peak of the most literary, the most artistic, the longest-established civilization that exists. It is a sister art to Chinese painting and Chinese ceramics, and therefore one would naturally expect to find in it a similar perfection of form and design, a like fluency and delicacy of expression, a like vivacity and force of idea and emotion, a like fusing of composite elements into a simplicity and workmanship which seem almost organic, a like mastery of craft, and a like concinnity and finish and exquisiteness of construction.

On the other hand, there can be no doubt that these qualities are entirely absent from the general run of poetic translations from the Chinese. The best that can be said of the best of them is that they have a quaint and piquant, rather rugged charm, like imitations, in wood-cut or literary composition, of *Ye Olde English*.

Poetic Translation

My first aim in making this book is to show to people who do not know Chinese that the Chinese can write poetry and how they write it. But this book is not an academic treatise. It is a book of poems and my intention is to make the translation of a poem to read like a poem itself. Accordingly, I do not comply with the modern fashion of putting Chinese verse into line by line prose, or into unmeasured sprung rhythm, which is the same thing. Besides, I believe that poetry cannot really be translated into prose. The translation of a poem into prose, which is merely verbally accurate, is not itself a poem and remains a crib. It misses the point and soul and reason of a poem, its specific beauty.

The superiority of poetic translations over prose ones is borne out by English literary history. The good translations of poetry which have been made in English were made by poets; by Chaucer, Spenser, Jonson, Dryden, Pope, Shelley, Fitzgerald. (Shelley's translations from the Greek are much closer to the letter as well as to the spirit of their originals than those by Richard Jebb and Gilbert Murray.)

Chinese poetry tends strongly to be epigrammatic, and most short Chinese poems are Epigrams. Now if an effective epigram is transformed into prose, it becomes inconsequential. For the point of epigrammatic and antithetical poetry (and Chinese poetry is both) is carried by its rhyme and rhythm. This is very clearly shown by taking any good epigram and de-rhyming it.

Balance and antithesis is of the essence of *all* Chinese art, and Chinese artistic unity is firmer than any other. Chinese poets always have observed the rules of Chinese rhetoric which are just slightly more streamlined than those of Greek rhetoric; and every Chinese poem has a point, firmly and tellingly driven home.

Versification

In an attempt to preserve the singing or musical quality in Chinese, I regularly employ rhyme. For instance, the last four lines of "A Patriot's Dream" by Lu Yu would be flat indeed without rhyme.

> Deep in the night, I heard a gale
> Roaring, and rain lashing;
> And dreamed there rode horsemen in mail,
> Through icy rivers splashing.

夜闌臥聽風吹雨，
鐵馬冰河入夢來！

It is unfair to Chinese poets, I believe, to render them into "Free

Verse". Their rhyming and metrical systems are more purely wrought and exquisite than any other. And the bulk of their poetry has in fact been written for music.

But rhyme presents its own special problems too. For instance, one feels that Li Po's (李白) "Night Thoughts" has to be translated (see p. 120). But every time I looked at it, the Cockney rhyme of *now*, *low* hit me between the eyes. It is the most difficult poem I ever tried. It is so simple and natural that translating it is like trying to dye a rose-leaf.

In Chinese the unit of rhythm is not the foot, or stressed plus unstressed syllable, but the syllable. A common characteristic of Chinese and Gaelic poets is their predilection for seven-syllabled and five-syllabled quatrain forms, with an interlaced pattern of sound that makes for "Unity in Variety". It could be made clear to English readers by reference to Shakespeare's heptasyllabics ('The Turtle and the Dove' and 'Orpheus with his lute made trees' [*Henry VIII*, III, i, 3], and songs in *The Tempest*). Pentasyllabics, on the other hand, are rare in English—and are very difficult to write—since they easily fall into a stark and terrible trochaic rhythm.

Then there are the tones. Translation of pitch and timbre (in the special sense of smoothness or non-smoothness of utterance) is a special feature of Chinese articulation. This variation, especially in timbre, is employed as a component of versification. The patterned interlacement of words of opposite pitch-and-timbre imparts to the poem a sort of poetical "fourth dimension", greatly increasing its power of expression and its concinnity, and making it approximate to music (in the strict sense of that word). Because of the importance of this musical dimension, sometimes lines have to be transposed for the sake of euphony (see p. 109, lines 5-6, 7-8).

For prosodic purposes, Chinese vocables are divided into two groups, of *smooth* (resounding, prolonged) syllables and *unsmooth* or *rough* (abrupt, vague, relatively harsh or jerky) syllables. "Smooth" and "unsmooth" are called "even" and "oblique" by English writers on Chinese, translating the terms in a literal manner. The poets adopted a criss-cross alternation of "smooth" and "unsmooth" syllables into the general structure of their verse. In Standard Tonal Verse, *shih* (詩), these are arranged in an antithetical, slightly asymmetrical order. The following, for example, is one of the patterns that a Chinese heptasyllabic Epigram may take (reading, as in ordinary English, from left to right):

> *Smooth smooth* rough rough rough *smooth smooth*
> Rough rough *smooth smooth* rough rough *smooth:*
> Rough rough *smooth smooth smooth* rough rough
> *Smooth smooth* rough rough rough *smooth smooth.*

A fair notion of what this pattern sounds like can be given in English by means of a slight *tour de main*, as in the following quatrain, where sonorous syllables are used for the Chinese 'smooth' syllables, and are italicized to make them quite clear. The rhyme system, which is the same as the Chinese, is that used in the *Rubáiyát*.

> *Cold lakes* shimmer at *noon-day*:
> By the *bleak shores* lovers *stray*.
> On my *gold lute, now* and then,
> *Sad tunes* of the south *I play*.

In order to catch the effect of these Chinese internal pitch-rhythms, I frequently use not only internal assonances, but also internal rhymes, especially when it is a case of carrying over some of the effect of that medial euphonic element 兮 . This inter-jection, *hsi* (Mandarin pronunciation), occurs so frequently it demands further explanation. In Cantonese, which preserves ancient sounds, it is pronounced like "Hi", lightly sighed—reminiscent of English literature's "*Heigh*-ho, *Hey* nonny nonny". It is sometimes joyous, sometimes sad. Other translators render this interjectional word as "O" or "ah". I rarely if ever do. This interjection is characteristic of *Ch'u Tz'u* (楚辭) and early Han poetry, and is sporadic in all dynasties. For instance, it occurs in each of the nine lines in Liu Ch'ê's (劉徹) "Lines on the Autumn Wind" (p.42); there I compensate for it by putting in double rhymes throughout the poem. (Waley in translating the same poem simply ignores it—as well as the original rhyme, of course; and the result is—complete flatness.)

Diction

Chinese has naturally its own specific modes of expression: its own metaphors and its own rhetorical forms. There are stock patterns of expression (which school-masters call idioms), and forceful original patterns which the individual writer invents. To discern the latter is certainly no easy thing; yet it is easy to know the former by the simple criterion of frequency in use. Now a forceful original mode of expression may be rendered into a forceful or usual form in English, but one may perhaps be mis-taken in regarding a fairly common Chinese combination as an unusual one: it is a mistake I have often made and corrected on better judgment. But a stock idiom or a stock metaphor cannot be obtruded as such into English. "As brave as a lion" may be wearisome, but it is English; "as brave as a tiger" is not.

Certain expressions must be altered. "Fair as jade" (applied to beautiful women) is a very charming metaphor in Chinese: but it cannot be put down in English (perhaps because jade connotes a worn-out taste and also a vulgar woman). "Moth-brow", as an epithet for fair ones, is both inaccurate and repugnant in English. It is inaccurate because the Chinese expression does not mean the brow of a moth, nor a brow like a moth, nor a brow like a moth's; it means moth-antenna. The word, before its application to a woman, is already metaphorical. As applied to a woman it means literally that her eyebrows have the dainty sweep of a moth's antennae. In fact it presupposes a concomitant loveliness. Thus when I translate,

> *The dainty-browed beloved one*
> *Before the horsemen dies*   (p.173)

the translation is accurate linguistically and, I hope, appropriate in the English context.

Similarly, in Tu Fu's (杜甫) poem "The Winsome Bride", (p. 142), "Fair as jade" is adequately rendered:

> *Sweet as a lily or a rose—*

the lily and rose being, in fact, terms of comparison for human loveliness, every bit as natural (I may say conventional) in English as jade is in Chinese.

In attempting to capture the elegant and refined nature of Chinese poetry, I had sometimes almost forgotten that affected simplicity and deliberate homeliness are characteristics of Chinese poetry. For instance, there is a quality vaguely reminiscent of ballad poetry that pervades the poetry of Tu Fu and other poets of his time. All true art is traditionary, Chinese not less so than any. In traditionary folklore, in old ballads and good modern ones, and in the work of great traditionary poets, there is a quality the Chinese call "flavour of antiquity", which might perhaps be more clearly described, in modern analytical fashion, as "psychological primitiveness". Poetry works with words, with their associations and suggestive "aura". You have the chivalrous poems of Spenser, the drawing-room poems of Pope, the political poems of Dryden, each with its apposite associative, suggestive words and phrases. But certain words and phrases have no associations but those which are primitive and therefore touch the heart most intimately.

The most convenient example I can find of this "psychological primitiveness" is a short poem (which is deliberately archaic), by an early T'ang poet, Sung Chih-wen (宋之問 660?-710), "Down the Mountain" 下山歌:

> Down, down the Lofty Mountain
>   (Many a time I sigh!)
> Hand in hand with a bonny person,
>   Step by step went I.
>
> The moon that shone between the pines
>   Is shining to this day:
> But never, never again, my dear,
>   Shall we go down that way.

> 下嵩山兮多所思，
> 携佳人兮步遲遲。
> 松間明月長如此，
> 君再遊兮復何時。

It may be noticed that in this poem every word and every phrase is primitive, and wakes a train of feeling that can only be described as primitive. Going down a mountain with a beloved person: 'hand in hand'. A feeling of instability and insecurity: 'step by step'. A solitude reaching back to the threshold of his race: 'The moon that shone between the pines'. And the primitive feeling behind all sad lyric poetry: 'never, never again, my dear'.

Tu Fu, like Shakespeare, spread his net wide, and used every device that came to his hand. This 'psychological primitiveness' is part of his art. It was also consonant with his character. He had a very kind heart and was fond of simple and old things. So it is not surprising that he should remind an English reader of 'the old song of Percy and Douglas'. I was once severely criticized for indulging in "off-key analogies", by which the reader presumably meant things like the incongruity of making a Tartar horseman cry out with a Scottish "och!" According to my critic, a particularly offensive translation was Han Shan's (寒山) "No Title":

> Old Jones who lived on the North Side
> Kept a most hospitable table:
> The night old Jones's missus died
> His house was thronged from floor to gable.
>
> But now old Jones himself is dead,
> No, not a tear for him is shed.
> From those who swilled his wines and food
> One would expect more gratitude.

> 城北仲家翁，
> 渠家多酒肉。
> 仲翁婦死時，
> 弔客滿堂屋。
> 仲翁自身亡，
> 能無一人哭。
> 喫他栢欒者，
> 何太冷心腹。

In fact, I do not like the poem much (though I believe it is perfectly translated—for what Touchstone is not faithful to his Audrey?), and it is by an obscure author. I was taken by its freakishness and lack of T'ang dynasty "augustness". And one of my "by-aims" in translating is to discount the prevalent notion that Chinese poetry is "august" and stodgy. In this case the poem is quite homely in the best sense of the word.

The translator also has to search for equivalents to archaic expressions of ancient Chinese poetry. There is, of course, justification for archaisms and even a grace in their use, if they can be smoothly introduced into a piece that is itself archaic. For instance, in a poem by Ch'ü Yüan (屈原) called the "Mountain Wraith", the first eight lines are representative:

> One may you see that haunts the mountain combe,
> In kirtle of clinging fig-leaves frocked, girdled with trailing dodders green.
> Lustrous-eyed is she, smiling fair;
> Of winsome mien and debonair.
> Her team of brinded panthers driving, followed by ratels streaked, she moves
> In chariot hewn of sapan-wood with flags of cinnamon,
> Wild dianthus all her gems, her braid of wintergreen,
> To gather posies of the field, a gift for him she loves.

> 若有人兮山之阿，
> 被薜荔兮帶女蘿。
> 既含睇兮又宜笑，
> 子慕予兮善窈窕。
> 乘赤豹兮徙文貍，
> 辛夷車兮結桂旗。
> 被石蘭兮帶杜衡，
> 折芳馨兮遺所思。

The poem is almost impossible to translate. It is bristling with *hapax legomena* and archaisms (even for 300 B.C.), and all through is interspersed with the interjection *hsi* 兮 (one for each of the twenty-seven lines). My translation attempts to match the original in every way: "Debonair" is the only translation of the Chinese epithet applied to this lady. She is queenly and elegant as well as winsome and weird. At every syllable I was striving to get "weird" sounds and effects corresponding to the "queerness" of the original. It is musical; so is the original. It is archaic and out of the mainstream of English writing; so are the *Ch'u Tz'u* archaic (gruesomely so). And being Southern songs, they are out of the mainstream of Chinese writing. Is the "Mountain Wraith" in its original form a bit "phoney"? I think so, but it makes a wonderful contrast to the clean primitiveness of the *Book of Poetry* and the robustious mouthings of the dynastic warriors that follow. Notice, for instance, the completely different tone in the following song of pure *braggadocio*, the "Great Wind Song" written by the first Han Emperor Liu Pang (劉邦):

> Brave hearts, sing ho!
>> Let the great wind blow,
>> The clouds are spread in flight.
> From hard campaign we are home again:
>> All the ground the oceans bound
>> Our glory hovers o'er.
> O where shall I find me men of might
>> To guard my frontiers four?

大風起兮雲飛揚，
威加海內兮歸故鄉，
安得猛士兮守四方。

Proper Names

Besides these intrinsic difficulties of translation, there are certain accidental difficulties. The chief one lies in the translation of proper names. For instance, it is impossible to translate

Chinese place names into English verse. The various systems of romanization that are employed for the rendering of Chinese have not lessened but accentuated the difficulty; whatever their degree of scientific accuracy, they are uniformly ugly. The truth is that a majority of monosyllabic sounds in English have either a vulgar or a trivial connotation. Chu Chin Chow, however one pronounces the name, will always look funny.

There are various ways of rectifying this difficulty. One is to avoid poems with proper names. An alternative is simply to omit proper names when they are not essential to the meaning. I do occasionally, though rarely, omit proper names when they are not really necessary and, at the same time, sound cacophonous in their barbarous English romanization. A good example is Li Po's "Farewell" (p. 116). The proper names of Yang-chow city and the Ch'ang-chiang river have been deliberately omitted.

> And so, dear friend, at Brown Crane Tower you,
> Bidding the West adieu,
> 'Mid April mists and blossoms go,
> Till in the vast blue-green
> Your lonely sail's far shade no more is seen,
> Only on the sky's verge the River's flow.

> 故人西辭黃鶴樓，
> 煙花三月下揚州。
> 孤帆遠影碧空盡，
> 惟見長江天際流。

Similarly in Tu Fu's "Gazing at the Great Mount" (p. 132), the first four lines of my translation read:

> To what shall I compare
> The Sacred Mount that stands,
> A balk of green that hath no end,
> Betwixt two lands!

岱宗夫如何？

齊魯青未了。

The proper names, *Tai-tsung* (one of the names given to T'ai-shan, the Sacred Mount, as a god), *Ch'i* and *Lu* (names of two ancient principalities) are left out.

But one may not omit those proper names (and they are many) which have an evocative connotation. For instance, Lo-yang (洛陽) has as important associations to a Chinese ear as Waterloo or Marathon to a Western ear. So another solution is to give the literal meaning or to use a periphrasis as short and graceful as one can manage when names are retained. Sometimes, especially with regard to a less known place name, one can translate the Chinese literally, as Sapphire Fields (藍田) or Wormwood Lane (蒿里). And even if the proper name can go into English one should often append an explanatory phrase (as the learned Milton so often did in his poetry). Two examples are found in Lin Hung's (林鴻) "On Wine" (p. 294). The first couplet reads:

> Confucianists that love old ways
> Forever prate of ancient glories.

儒生好奇古，

出口談唐虞。

Ancient glories: this phrase replaces the author's T'ang (唐) and Yü (虞), a reference to two pre-historic legendary worthies, whose names would mean nothing to an English reader. This second couplet:

> Where, if they lived in ancient days,
> Should they find matter for their stories?

21

倘生羲皇前，
所談竟何如？

Lived in ancient days: Literally, "lived before Hsi Huang", the first legendary Emperor, which again would be meaningless in English. An equivalent translation would be, "before the days of Adam" (or Noah, or Methuselah), but this would be altogether incongruous.

For scenic Chiang-nan (江南), which one cannot evade, I have used the original meaning of the expression, "South of the River" or else the more accurately-coined expression, "South River Land", as in Po Chü-i's (白居易) poem, "Remembering South River Land" (p. 188).

There is a similar difficulty as regards the names of plants which have no English name or else a hideous commercial one. The beautiful *Wu-t'ung* or Phoenix Tree (梧桐樹) is ineptly called by some the *T'ung*-tree, which reminds one of "the land where the Bong tree grows".

In sum, all Chinese poetry is concinnate, polished, vivid, formal, forceful, dramatic and rhetorical. As mentioned above, I mean rhetorical in the Chinese sense of the word; that is, the art of elegant diction. The well-known lines of Gautier (who apparently knew something of Chinese poetry and admired it):

> *Oui, l'oeuvre sort plus belle*
> *D'une forme au travail*
> *Rebelle:*
> *Vers, marbre, onyx, émail*

might well be chosen as a motto or emblem for the splendid eras of Chinese poetry this anthology attempts to represent.

List of Poems

25

26

27

30

31

關雎

關關雎鳩，在河之洲。

窈窕淑女，君子好逑。

參差荇菜，左右流之。

窈窕淑女，寤寐求之。

求之不得，寤寐思服。

悠哉悠哉，輾轉反側。

參差荇菜，左右采之。

窈窕淑女，琴瑟友之。

參差荇菜，左右芼之。

窈窕淑女，鐘鼓樂之。

ANONYMOUS[1]

Book of Poetry, Chou dynasty

Courtship Song

Sea-hawks are calling[2]
By the river-board.
A modest sweet maid
Is to wed a lord.

Sprayey Floating Hearts[3]
Trail we left and right.
A modest sweet maid
He seeks dark and light.

Seeking her in vain,
Dark and light he yearns,
Longing, aye longing,
He tosses and turns.

Sprayey Floating Hearts
Cull we left and right.
A modest sweet maid
Lute and harp invite.

Sprayey Floating Hearts
Left and right we tell.
A modest sweet maid
Welcome drum and bell.

靜女

靜女其姝，俟我于城隅。

愛而不見，搔首踟躕。

靜女其孌，貽我彤管。

彤管有煒，說懌女美。

自牧歸荑，洵美且異。

匪女之爲美，美人之貽。

ANONYMOUS

Book of Poetry, Chou dynasty

That Gentle Maid

That gentle maid so sweet
Said by the curtain-wall we'd meet.
Then as I came she hid away,
To leave me moping in dismay.

That gentle maid so free,
A crimson reed she gave to me.
O crimson reed, so fresh, so bright,
To gaze at thee brings much delight.

This meadow reed from her,
Never was seen a daintier.
Yet not for daintiness I care:
'Tis Beauty's giving makes it fair.

桃夭

桃之夭夭，灼灼其華。

之子于歸，宜其室家。

桃之夭夭，有蕡其實。

之子于歸，宜其家室。

桃之夭夭，其葉蓁蓁。

之子于歸，宜其家人。

Wedding Song

Peach-tree so tender,
With blossoms aglow.
These pretty maidens
A-wedding must go.
Joy may they take
In the home they shall make.

Peach-tree so tender
With fruit heavy-laden.
Off to be wedded
Is each pretty maiden.
Fair fall her lot
In the home she has got.

Peach-tree so tender
With leaves for a cover.
Each pretty maiden
Is off with her lover.
Dear be the home
To the which she shall come.

草　蟲

喓喓草蟲，趯趯阜螽。

未見君子，憂心忡忡。

亦既見止，亦既覯止，

我心則降。

陟彼南山，言采其蕨。

未見君子，憂心惙惙。

亦既見止，亦既覯止，

我心則說。

陟彼南山，言采其薇。

未見君子，我心傷悲。

亦既見止，亦既覯止，

我心則夷。

ANONYMOUS

Book of Poetry, Chou dynasty

While Locusts Sang[4]

While locusts sang
And locusts played;
My love being gone,
My heart was sad.
But once I spy him
And once I'm nigh him,
My heart is glad.

I climbed yon hill
To gather fern:[5]
My love being gone,
My heart was torn.
But once I spy him
And once I'm nigh him,
No more I'll mourn.

I climbed yon hill
To pluck wild pease:
My love being gone,
I knew no ease.
But once I spy him
And once I'm nigh him,
My grief will cease.

猗蘭操

習習谷風，以陰以雨。

之子于歸，遠送於野。

何彼蒼天，不得其所。

逍遙九州，無所定處。

時人闇蔽，不知賢者。

年紀逝邁，一身將老。

ANONYMOUS

often attributed to Confucius

551-479 B.C., Age of Spring and Autumn

Disappointment[6]

Through the mild breeze,
In cloud and rain,
Across the weald
I ride again:
(O mighty Heav'n!)
To roam unblest
The Regions Nine
And find no rest.
Benighted souls
Ignore the Sage;
While the long years
Bring on old age.

劉　徹

秋風辭

秋風起兮白雲飛，

草木黃落兮鴈南歸。

蘭有秀兮菊有芳，

懷佳人兮不能忘。

汎樓船兮濟汾河，

橫中流兮揚素波。

簫鼓鳴兮發櫂歌，

歡樂極兮哀情多。

少壯幾時兮奈老何。

LIU CH'Ê[7]

165-87 B.C., Han dynasty

Lines on the Autumn Wind

The autumn blast is rising fast:
    White clouds are scudding free.
Green hill and vale grow sere and pale,
    And wild geese southward flee.
Chrysanthemum and orchid[8] bloom
    Blow sweetly at the full—
And never let me thee forget,
    My Lady beautiful!
Our high-pooped barge glides by the marge
    Of tributary flume:[9]
Breasting the maze of floods we raise
    A crest of creamy spume.
Drumming and noise of clear hautboys
    Chime with the oarsmen's song.
When all delight has reached its height,
    Then sorrows thick will throng.
Youth holds a lease that soon must cease:
    No mortal life is long.

悲愁歌

吾家嫁我兮天一方，
遠託異國兮烏孫王。
穹廬爲室兮氈爲牆，
以肉爲食兮酪爲漿。
居常土思兮心內傷，
願爲黃鵠兮歸故鄉。

LIU HSI-CHÜN

flor. 100 B.C.

Lamentation

My folk have wedded me
    Across heaven's span,
Into a far country,
    To a Turkish Khan.
A black tent is our hall,
    With felt for party wall:
Flesh is our nutriment,
    And cheese for condiment.
So homesick here — would I
    From this lothly band
Like the Brown Swan might fly
    To my native land!

贈婦詩

蕭蕭僕夫征，鏘鏘揚和鈴。

清晨當引邁，束帶待雞鳴。

顧看空室中，髣髴想姿形。

一別懷萬恨，起坐爲不寧。

何用敘我心，遺思致欵誠。

寶釵好耀首，明鏡可鑒形。

芳香去垢穢，素琴有清聲。

詩人感木瓜，乃欲答瑤瓊。

愧彼贈我厚，慙此往物輕。

雖知未足報，貴用敘我情。

CH'IN CHIA

flor. 150 A.D.

A Farewell Poem for His Absent Wife

Hurriedly drives the charioteer.
Merrily ring the shaft-bells clear.
'Tis peep of dawn, and time to go.
Belted and girt to meet cock-crow,
Back at our empty quarters glancing,
I seem to see your form entrancing.
A thousand woes at this leave-taking
Vex my mind, asleep or waking.[10]
What token shall I leave of love,
My faith and tenderness to prove?
A costly pin[11] your head to grace:
A mirror quaint to light your face:
Perfume all that's foul expelling:
Snow-white lute of tone excelling.
His debt to quit, a rosy sàrd
For quince returned the ancient bard.[12]
I, when I think of all you've given,
Blush for the bargain all uneven.
Slight though the gift be; you must know
Somewhat it serves my love to show.

孔　融

雜詩

遠送新行客，歲暮乃來歸。

入門望愛子，妻妾向人悲。

聞子不可見，日已潛光輝。

孤墳在西北，常念君來遲。

褰裳上墟丘，但見蒿與薇。

白骨歸黃泉，肌體乘塵飛。

生時不識父，死後知我誰。

孤魂游窮暮，飄飄安所依。

人生圖嗣息，爾死我念追。

俛仰內傷心，不覺淚沾衣。

人生自有命，但恨生日希。

My Son

Abroad I did a friend accompany,
And till the year's decline was I delayed.
As home I entered my sweet son to see,
The womenfolk a doleful outcry made.
They told me I should never see my child:
The splendour of the day was sunk in gloom.
"His little grave is in the Northwest wild."
"How sad we were," they said, "you could not come!"
I girt myself and climbed the lonely mound
Where ferns and wormwood only met the eye.
His bones are in their place beneath the ground,
His flesh and frame blown with the dust on high.
You that in life did never father know,
How shall you know me when my days are ended?
In twilight grim my ghost unblest must go,
All at a loss, unhallowed, unattended.[13]
What mortal does not crave continuance
Of breed? As on your death I pondered there,
A spasm of sorrow shook my inmost sense
And tears bedrenched my garment unaware.
We know that life and death are ruled by fate.
Ah yes—but you were here so short a date!

疾邪詩二首

一

河清不可俟，

人命不可延。

順風激靡草，

富貴者稱賢。

文籍雖滿腹，

不如一囊錢。

伊優北堂上，

骯髒倚門邊。

Poems of Disgust

i

Life is not long enough, I fear
To see the turbid River clear.

As light grass in the wind is swayed,
To rich and great is honour paid.

What though with lore thy belly sags:
Lore is outweighed by money-bags.

Obsequiousness is glorified:
While honest worth must wait outside.

二

勢家多所宜，

欬唾自成珠。

被褐懷金玉，

蘭蕙化爲芻。

賢者雖獨悟，

所困在羣愚。

且各守爾分，

勿復空馳驅。

哀哉復哀哉，

此是命矣夫。

All venerate our dukes and earls:
Their spittle is esteemed as pearls.

Pure gold in hodden grey is hid:
And orchid sweet for straw is chid.

Though none but sages truth can know:
Yet these to vulgar fools must bow.

Well, it remains our lot to bide,
Nor strive in vain against the tide.

Yet woe is me and woe again
That such should be the state of men!

薤　露

薤上露，
何易晞。
露晞明朝更復落，
人死一去何時歸。

ANONYMOUS

Royal Conservatory, Western Han dynasty

The Dew That on Shallot-leaves Lies[14]

How soon in sunlight dries
The dew that on shallot-leaves lies!
Yet the same dew,
Though now 'tis dry,
Tomorrow morn will fall anew.
But when shall mortal men,
If once they die,
Ever return again?

長歌行

青青園中葵，朝露待日晞。

陽春布德澤，萬物生光輝。

常恐秋節至，焜黃華葉衰。

百川東到海，何時復西歸。

少壯不努力，老大徒傷悲。

ANONYMOUS

Royal Conservatory, Western Han dynasty

"Long-song Lay"[15]

Green are the garden mallows! Soon
    The morning dews will be a-drying.
Though wide the blithe Spring shed his boon,
    A radiant world revivifying:
Yet dread I Autumn's coming on,
    —Sere yellow leaves of blossoms flying.
Our brooks that eastward reach the sea,[16]
    When to the West shall they return?
If Youth in sloth should wasted be,
    Old Age can only grieve and mourn.

迢迢牽牛星

迢迢牽牛星，皎皎河漢女。
纖纖擢素手，札札弄機杼。
終日不成章，泣涕零如雨。
河漢清且淺，相去復幾許。
盈盈一水間，脈脈不得語。

ANONYMOUS

Eastern Han dynasty

Far in the Skies Is the Cowherd Star[17]

Far in the skies is the Cowherd Star:
Bright on the Milky Way the Maid
Lightly her snowy fingers raises,
Jogging her shuttle through its mazes.
But her stint of work is never-ending,
And her tears like sobbing showers descending.
Though clear and shallow the Milky Way,
Never they'll meet for many a day.
No word she says, but stares dismayed,
Alone by that surging River far.

生年不滿百

生年不滿百，常懷千歲憂。

晝短苦夜長，何不秉燭游。

爲樂當及時，何能待來玆。

愚者愛惜費，但爲後世嗤。

仙人王子喬，難可與等期。

ANONYMOUS

Eastern Han dynasty

Life That's Scarce
a Hundred Years

Life, that's scarce a hundred years,
Holds millenniums of fears.
Brief its noon, and long its night:
Best then mingle dark with light.
Merry-making whiles ye may:
Wait not for another day.
Fools that treasure up their stock
After-generations mock.
Him that held a bond with fate[18]
None may seek to emulate.

龜雖壽

神龜雖壽，猶有竟時。

螣蛇乘霧，終爲土灰。

老驥伏櫪，志在千里。

烈士暮年，壯心不已。

盈縮之期，不但在天。

養怡之福，可得永年。

TS'AO TS'AO[19]

155-220, Wei dynasty

The Indomitable Soul

Though old be the wise tortoise, yet
    Die in the end he must:
And the mist-scaling dragonet,
    He too shall come to dust.

Yet ancient steeds in stall that lie
    Dream of the leagues they ran:
And heroes, though their doom is nigh,
    As ever play the man;

For the attainment of our ends
    Rests not with Heaven alone.
The joy that strength of soul attends
    Through endless years lives on.

雜詩

南國有佳人，容華若桃李。
朝游江北岸，夕宿瀟湘沚。
時俗薄朱顏，誰爲發皓齒。
俛仰歲將暮，榮耀難久恃。

TS'AO CHIH[20]

192-232

Allegory

In the South a lady hied,
Fair as springtime blossoms sweet,
At morn from the North Bank, to bide
At eve in Isle where Waters Meet.

Vulgar eyes her vermeil roses
Scorn, nor heed her song so free.
Soon, too soon, as the year closes,
Her loveliness will cease to be.

贈從弟

亭亭山上松，瑟瑟谷中風。
風聲一何盛，松枝一何勁。
冰霜正慘悽，終歲常端正。
豈不罹凝寒，松柏有本性。

LIU CHÊN
?-217

For His Cousin

See the gaunt mountain-pine
Above the wind-swept vale!
Wild as the gale may whine,
Its boughs no moment quail.

When frost and ice lie drear,
They stand the whole year long:
They feel not coldness near,
The pine and cedar strong.

秋胡行二首

一

富貴尊榮，憂患諒獨多。

富貴尊榮，憂患諒獨多。

古人所懼，豐屋蔀家。

人害其上，獸惡雀羅。

惟有貧賤，可以無他。

歌以言之，富貴憂患多。

Songs of Disillusionment

i

Honour and glory
Breed care and worry.
Fame and success
Mean much distress.
On lofty state
Will ruin wait,
Ev'n as a net
For beasts is set;
While poor and mean
Abide serene.
Therefore I may
Both sing and say:
Honour and glory
Breed care and worry.

二

絕智棄學，游心於玄默。

絕智棄學，游心於玄默。

遇過而悔，當不自得。

垂釣一壑，所樂一國。

被髮行歌，和者四塞。

歌以言之，游心於玄默。

Wisdom and learning I abhor:
Wander, my soul, in Quietude!
Wisdom and learning I detest:
In Quietude I set my rest:
Repenting what may be amiss,
All my ambition, all my bliss,
To trail my hook by some ravine,
Lord of a kingdom quite unseen.
And so, bare-headed as I go,
Though all around are scenes of woe,
This be my song for evermore:
Wander, my soul, in Quietude!

陶　潛

桃花源記

晉太元中，武陵人捕魚爲業，緣溪行，忘路之遠近。忽逢桃花林，夾岸數百步，中無雜樹，芳草鮮美，落英繽紛。漁人甚異之。復前行，欲窮其林。林盡水源，便得一山。山有小口，髣髴若有光。便捨船，從口入。初極狹，纔通人，復行數十步，豁然開朗。土地平曠，屋舍儼然，有良田美池桑竹之屬。阡陌交通，雞犬相聞。其中往來種作，男女衣著，悉如外人。黃髮垂髫，並怡然自樂。見漁人，乃大驚，問所從來。具答之。便要還家，設酒殺雞作食。

T'AO CH'IEN[21]

365-427, Chin dynasty

Peach-blossom Fount[22]

PREFACE

During the reign period T'ai-yuan [376-396] of the Chin dynasty, a man of Wu-ling who plied the fisher's trade, losing all count of distance as he made his way along a certain brook, suddenly came on a grove of peach-trees in blossom which fringed the shore some hundred paces, no other trees interspersed, where on scented grasses fresh and pleasing to the eye lay fallen blossoms in gay profusion, at sight of which the fisherman was much amazed. He went on farther, hoping to traverse the grove; which ended at a fount of water above which a hill rose. In the hillside was a small opening from which light seemed to glimmer. So he left his boat and entered at the opening, which at first was exceeding narrow, barely wide enough to allow of passage. When he had proceeded some little way, all at once there was a glow of dazzling light. Over a broad expanse of land, dotted at due intervals with houses and dwellings, were goodly holdings with fair pools, set with mulberries, bamboos and the like; the fields intersected by regular paths, and the sound of farmyard animals within earshot. There did they go about their farming, men and women arrayed as it were in alien attire; while aged men and infants merrily disported themselves. At sight of the fisherman, much startled, they inquired whence he had come. When he had replied, nothing would satisfy them but to receive him in their homes; and wine they broached and poultry killed for his entertainment. As they of the villages heard of his coming, they flocked to make their

73

村中聞有此人，咸來問訊。自云先世避秦時亂，率妻子邑人來此絕境，不復出焉，遂與外人間隔。問今是何世，乃不知有漢，無論魏晉。此人一一為具言所聞，皆歎惋。餘人各復延至其家，皆出酒食。停數日，辭去。此中人語云，不足為外人道也。既出，得其船，便扶向路，處處誌之。及郡下，詣太守說如此。太守即遣人隨其往，尋向所誌，遂迷不復得路。南陽劉子驥，高尚士也，聞之，欣然規往。未果，尋病終。後遂無問津者。

桃花源詩

嬴氏亂天紀，賢者避其世。
黃綺之商山，伊人亦云逝。

interrogations. By them he was informed how in a former age, fleeing the terror and confusion of the Ch'in regime, leading their families and fellow-townsmen, they had come to this untenanted spot away from the inhabited world, never to issue forth again. They asked what royal family was now in power,—knowing nothing as they did of the Han reign, not to speak of the succeeding dynasties of Wei and Chin. As he in his turn replied to their several questions, they expressed a rueful wonderment. One by one the rest invited him to banquet in their homes, and regaled him with store of wine and viands. After the lapse of some days he took his departure. Among his hosts there were those who reminded him that it might be wiser if one spoke not to strangers of their affairs. Emerging once more, he found his boat and retraced the way he came, marking as he did so each various point of his journey. Arriving at his own district, he betook himself to the Prefect of the locality and recounted what had befallen; who forthwith despatched certain ones to accompany him in search of the place he had described. They were at a loss, however, to rediscover the route. Liu Tzu-chi, an eminent worthy of Nan-yang, having heard the story, made eager preparation to voyage thither: but all to no effect, for he died of illness on his quest. Nor in later times was further inquiry made.

POEM

When the First Emperor[23] foiled Heaven's decree,
All honest men respued his tyranny.
A knot of nobles to the lone hills fled:
In time 'twas given out that they were dead.

往跡浸復湮，來逕遂蕪廢。

相命肆農耕，日入從所憩。

桑竹垂餘蔭，菽稷隨時藝。

春蠶收長絲，秋熟靡王稅。

荒路曖交通，雞犬互鳴吠。

俎豆猶古法，衣裳無新製。

童孺縱行歌，斑白歡游詣。

草榮識節和，木衰知風厲。

雖無紀曆誌，四時自成歲。

怡然有餘樂，于何勞智慧。

奇蹤隱五百，一朝敞神界。

淳薄既異源，旋復還幽蔽。

借問游方士，焉測塵囂外。

願言躡輕風，高舉尋吾契。

Their former track with mists was shrouded deep:
The path they traversed overgrown and steep.
Shoulder by shoulder did they plant and till,
And as the sun went down might rest their fill
'Neath verdurous shade of drooping mulberry-trees,
Thus as they willed they sowed their corn and pease:
In spring they wound long threads their silk-worms spun;
At harvest Royal taxes paid they none.
By lonely ways from traffic far retired
Only the noise of dogs and fowl was heard.
In ritual they kept the ancient way,
Nor changed their dress's mode from day to day.
There did small children frolic make and song,
And old men merrily saunter all day long.
By grasses lush they knew the season mild;
And weary trees presaged when winds blew wild.
What though they kept no count of months or days,
Still the four seasons made one year always.
In blissful state of seeming-endless joy,
What need their brains with knowledge to annoy?
Five hundred years uncouth they dimly stayed
Till did a wight their fairy land invade;
But, such the vagueness of the hidden spring,
Thenceforth were spared from curious visiting.
How should the journeyman with wares for sale
Fathom the secret of this sylvan vale?
O would that I, snatching some gentle wind,
Might hoist my sail and there true kinship find!

北朝樂府民歌

一　瑯琊王歌

新買五尺刀，懸著中梁柱。
一日三摩娑，劇於十五女。

二　企喻歌

男兒欲作健，結伴不須多。
鷂子經天飛，羣雀兩向波。

ANONYMOUS

Northern Dynasty

Border Songs

i

The five-foot sword I now possess,
   Hung in the midmost colonnade,
Thrice in a day do I caress:
   Never did man so love a maid.

ii

To have store of allies
   Is no great matter.
When the sparrow-hawk flies,
   The small birds scatter.

隋煬帝時挽舟者歌

我兄征遼東，餓死青山下。
今我挽龍舟，又困隋隄道。
方今天下饑，路糧無些小。
前去三千程，此身安可保。
寒骨枕荒沙，幽魂泣煙草。
悲損門內妻，望斷吾家老。
安得義男兒，焚此無主屍。
引其孤魂回，負其白骨歸。

ANONYMOUS

Sui dynasty

Barge-hauler's Song [24]

My brother on a far campaign
Of hunger 'neath the dark hills died.
I haul the Royal Barge amain
Along the Royal Causeway's side.
Throughout the kingdom famine rages,
For victuals scant we toil and strive.
Think you, another thousand stages,
What chance have I to keep alive?
Chill bones lapped in desert sands,
Ghost in foggy grasses wailing,
Woe worth the wife who waiting stands,
And parents' sorrow unavailing!
Be it granted some gallant friend,
Burning this corpse untenanted,
May house the wandering soul, and send
My ashes home when I am dead!

在獄詠蟬

西陸蟬聲唱，南冠客思深。

不堪玄鬢影，來對白頭吟。

露重飛難進，風多響易沉。

無人信高潔，誰爲表予心。

LO PIN-WANG

640?-684?, T'ang dynasty

To a Cicada from Prison[25]

As autumn falls and the cicada's song
Trills, the poor thrall more deeply feels his wrong.
No more of this, little black-membraned shade!
Play not thy music near my hairs so white.
The heavy dews will only clog thy flight,
And by the winds thy bourdoning be laid.
None will give credence to the innocent:
So none can prove the truth of my intent.

回鄉偶書

少小離家老大回，
鄉音無改鬢毛衰。
兒童相見不相識，
笑問客從何處來。

HO CHIH-CHANG

659-744

Homecoming

*—jotted down on returning home
after long separation*

Of youth bereft as home I came—alas,
With brogue unchanged but sadly altered hair;
My children wondered who the stranger was.
They smiled and said: "Where do you come from, sir?"

石 召

早行遇雪

荒郊昨夜雪，

羸馬又須行。

四顧無人迹，

雞鳴第一聲。

SHIH CHAO

T'ang dynasty

Snow at Morning

Out on the moors it snowed all night;
    And yet my nag must go.
No sign of human life in sight,
    One hears the first cock crow.

湖口望廬山瀑布水

萬丈紅泉落，

迢迢半紫氛。

奔流下雜樹，

灑落出重雲。

日照虹霓似，

天清風雨聞。

靈山多秀色，

空水共氤氳。

CHANG CHIU-LING

673-740

The Waterfall

Out of the mists and the clouds with a leap and a
    shuddering cry
The waterfall, red with the blood of the earth, crashes
    to death with a sigh,
Down past the shivering trees to the rocks where its
    waters die
To arise in a vapour of ghostly forms seeking again the
    sky.
They weave from the threads of the sun a rainbow of
    tremulous light
While the sound of their dying sighs is the voice of a
    storm in its might.
The mountains in beauty dressed stand awed by that
    magical sight
Of the wedding of Heaven and earth in a waterfall's
    headlong flight.

李隆基

經魯祭孔子而歎之

夫子何爲者，

栖栖一代中。

地猶鄹氏邑，

宅即魯王宮。

歎鳳嗟身否，

傷麟怨道窮。

今看兩楹奠，

當與夢時同。

LI LUNG-CHI[26]

685-762

To Confucius

—uttered under stress of emotion, as he sacrificed to Confucius while passing through the ancient kingdom of Lu

Master, what were you about,
Wandering an age throughout?
Still the land from which you came
Bears its ancient townsfolk's name:
And the house wherein you played,
Kings of Lu a palace made.
For the Phoenix did you mourn
Ill the day that you were born,
For the Unicorn felt pain,
Knowing that your work was vain.
See by yonder colonnade
Sacrificial vessels laid.
May not this be rightly deemed
Equal to the dream you dreamed?

春　曉

春眠不覺曉，
處處聞啼鳥。
夜來風雨聲，
花落知多少。

MÊNG HAO-JAN[27]
689-740

Dawn in Spring

How suddenly the morning comes in Spring!
On every side you hear the sweet birds sing.
Last night amidst the storm—Ah, who can tell,
With wind and rain, how many blossoms fell?

夜歸鹿門歌

山寺鳴鐘晝已昏，漁梁渡頭爭渡喧。

人隨沙岸向江村，余亦乘舟歸鹿門。

鹿門月照開煙樹，忽到龐公棲隱處。

巖扉松逕長寂寥，唯有幽人自來去。

Home to Deer-Gate at Night

A mountain temple tolls the end of day;
At Weir-Bridge Ford late crowds vociferate;
Along the sands they take their homeward way,
And I sail in my boat home to Deer-Gate.

The Deer-Gate moon shines on a forest haze:
Here is the site the Ancient Hermit chose:
Through rocky door and silent pine-fringed ways
Only the solitary comes and goes.

登鸛雀樓

白日依山盡，
黃河入海流。
欲窮千里目，
更上一層樓。

WANG CHIH-HUAN

695-?

On Top of Stork-bird Tower

As daylight fades along the hill,
The Yellow River joins the sea.
To gaze unto infinity,
Go mount another storey still.

宿龍興寺

香剎夜忘歸，
松清古殿扉。
燈明方丈室，
珠繫比丘衣。
白日傳心淨，
青蓮喻法微。
天花落不盡，
處處鳥銜飛。

CH'I MU-CH'IEN

flor. 726

Night at Lung-hsing Monastery

Tarrying in this sweet-scented fane one felt not it was
night,
Where purest pines by the rude doors of ancient halls
arose,
Till from the prior's chamber bright
There fell a light
On beads that hang as ropes of pearl from beggar bonzes'
clothes.

Here day's last rays bring to the soul a peace celestial:
Those great green lilies are a sign of wisdom's gaze pro-
found.
Nor have the Heavenly Maidens all
Their flowers let fall:
Each with a blossom in his bill, birds flutter all around.

破山寺後禪院

清晨入古寺，初日照高林。
曲徑通幽處，禪房花木深。
山光悅鳥性，潭影空人心。
萬籟此俱寂，惟聞鐘磬音。

CH'ANG CHIEN

flor. 727

Hermitage at
Broken-Hill Monastery

Within this convent old
By the clear dawn
Tall woods are lit with earliest rays.
Lo, here and there a pathway strays
On to a hidden lawn
Whose flowery thickets cells enfold.

The light upon yon hill
Lulls every bird;
And shadows on dark tarns set free
The souls of men from vanity.
Each sound of earth is still,
Only the temple bell is heard.

王　維

青　谿

言入黃花川，每逐青谿水。

隨山將萬轉，趣途無百里。

聲喧亂石中，色靜深松裏。

漾漾汎菱荇，澄澄映葭葦。

我心素已閒，清川澹如此。

請留盤石上，垂釣將已矣。

WANG WEI[28]

701-761

Green Brook

Along by Yellow-Blossom Beck
To Green Brook as you cross and tack;
Turn after turn the hills you coast,
A voyage of ten miles at most.
A babel of waves on boulders whines,
Where hues are still beneath green pines
Blue water-bloom and river-bud
Wide are hurried adown the flood:
And reeds and bulrushes appear
In limpid waters mirrored clear.
So long have I been fancy-free,
So dear this stream's simplicity:
Here on some stone slab could I stay,
Rod in hand, for ever and aye.

竹里館

獨坐幽篁裏，
彈琴復長嘯。
深林人不知，
明月來相照。

WANG WEI

In Bamboo-Alley Grange

Alone in tall secluded groves I lie,
To play upon my lute or by and by
Loud chant. In woodlands deep where none may see,
Comes the fair moon and sheds her light on me.

閨　怨

閨中少婦不知愁，

春日凝妝上翠樓。

忽見陌頭楊柳色，

悔敎夫壻覓封侯。

Regret

A lady fair that nothing knows of care
    In bright array
    On a springtime day
Mounts to the tower of her leaf-emerald bower.

Sudden she sees the wayside willow trees
    In light hues clad:
    And her heart is sad—
She bade her lord win glory of the sword.

李　白

下終南山過斛斯山人宿置酒

暮從碧山下，山月隨人歸。

卻顧所來徑，蒼蒼橫翠微。

相攜及田家，童稚開荊扉。

綠竹入幽徑，青蘿拂行衣。

歡言得所憩，美酒聊共揮。

長歌吟松風，曲盡河星稀。

我醉君復樂，陶然共忘機。

LI PO[29]

701-762

Down from the Mountain

As down Mount Emerald at eve I came,
  The mountain moon went all the way with me.
Backward I looked, to see the heights aflame
  With a pale light that glimmered eerily.[31]

A little lad undid the rustic latch
  As hand in hand your cottage we did gain,[32]
Where green limp tendrils at our cloaks did catch,[33]
  And dim bamboos o'erhung a shadowy lane.

Gaily I cried, "Here may we rest our fill!"
  Then choicest wines we quaffed; and cheerily
"The Wind among the Pines" we sang, until
  A few faint stars hung in the Galaxy.[34]

  Merry were you, my friend: and drunk was I,[35]
  Blissfully letting all the world go by.

李　白

清平調三首

一

雲想衣裳花想容，
春風拂檻露華濃。
若非羣玉山頭見，
會向瑤臺月下逢。

LI PO

Yang Kuei-fei and the Peony-rose

i

In clouds I see those garments, and
   In the flowers that face.
With springtime winds at casement fann'd,
   Heavenly dews breathe grace.
If not on hills ruled by the Fairy Queen
     By moonlight else
     In magic dells
Such beauties might be seen.

二

一枝紅豔露凝香，

雲雨巫山枉斷腸。

借問漢宮誰得似，

可憐飛燕倚新妝。

三

名花傾國兩相歡，

長得君王帶笑看。

解釋春風無限恨，

沈香亭北倚闌干。

Let spring of rosy loveliness
    Dewy sweets distil:
Then mourn no more for love's distress
    Bride of Mystic Hill.[36]
By what dead fair may these be typified?
      "Flying Swallow"[37]
      Might they follow
When in her height of pride.

iii

Fam'd flower! Ravisher of kings!
    Like is their delight.
Tender smile to monarch brings
    Each or either's sight.
Glooms that under zephyrs lower
      Are borne away
      While bide he may
North of "Embalmed Bower".

李　白

春日醉起言志

處世若大夢，胡爲勞其生。

所以終日醉，頽然臥前楹。

覺來盼庭前，一鳥花間鳴。

借問此何日，春風語流鶯。

感之欲歎息，對酒還自傾。

浩歌待明月，曲盡已忘情。

A Homily on Ideals in Life,
Uttered in Springtime on Rising
From a Drunken Slumber

Since Life is but a Dream,
Why toil to no avail?
Therefore it is that drunk all day
Listless beneath my porch I lay.
Waking, across the lawn I peer.
A bird from out the blossoms cried.
Tell me what season of the year,
What day may this day be?
'Twas a chance oriole
That babbled on the springtime gale.
At thought of which I all but sighed:
But then again addressed me to my bowl;
And sang with mighty din
To usher the moon in.
And now my song is done—Ay me,
I have forgot the theme.

李　白

送孟浩然之廣陵

故人西辭黃鶴樓，
煙花三月下揚州。
孤帆遠影碧空盡，
惟見長江天際流。

Farewell

*—on seeing Mêng Hao-jan off from
Brown Crane Tower as he took
his departure for Kuang-ling*

And so, dear friend, at Brown Crane Tower you,
   Bidding the West adieu,
  'Mid April mists and blossoms go,
   Till in the vast blue-green
Your lonely sail's far shade no more is seen,
Only on the sky's verge the River's flow.

李 白

望廬山瀑布

日照香爐生紫煙，
遙看瀑布掛長川。
飛流直下三千尺，
疑是銀河落九天。

Cascade

—gazing at the cascade on Lu Shan

Where crowns a purple haze
Ashimmer in sunlight rays
The hill called Incense-Burner Peak, from far
To see, hung o'er the torrent's wall,
That waterfall
Vault sheer three thousand feet, you'd say
The Milky Way
Was tumbling from the high heavens, star on star.

李　白

夜　思

牀前明月光，
疑是地上霜。
舉頭望明月，
低頭思故鄉。

Night Thoughts[38]

As by my bed
The moon did beam,
It seemed as if with frost the earth were spread.
But soft I raise
My head, to gaze
At the fair moon. And now,
With head bent low,
Of home I dream.

古朗月行 節錄

小時不識月，

呼作白玉盤。

又疑瑤臺鏡，

飛在碧雲端。

The Moon

When I was very small,
    Sometimes I used to call
The moon in heaven a jade-white soup tureen;
    Sometimes I thought it was
    A sort of magic glass,
Flying across cloudbanks of pale blue-green.

李 白

宣州謝朓樓餞別校書叔雲

棄我去者，昨日之日不可留。

亂我心者，今日之日多煩憂。

長風萬里送秋雁，

對此可以酣高樓。

蓬萊文章建安骨，

中間小謝又清發。

俱懷逸興壯思飛，

欲上青天攬明月。

At a Banquet Held in Hsieh T'iao's Tower in Hsüanchou, to bid farewell to Archivist Shu Yün

Ah, my betrayer!
Yesterday's day that never will return.
Ah, my dismayer!
This day today that makes me this day mourn.
Now autumn geese down the long winds are borne,
Come let us drink! Drinking may make us gayer.

Of writings in your fairy store
The last of Han we count the core.
And among them, most fresh of thought
Are those that little Hsieh has wrought.
Like him a fluent vein you hold;
Like his a mounting spirit bold.
Fain would you climb the azure sky
To clasp yon moon that shines on high.

抽刀斷水水更流，
舉杯消愁愁更愁。
人生在世不稱意，
明朝散髮弄扁舟。

Go take your sword and waters cleave:
The waters yet will flow.
Go lift your cup, the less to grieve:
Grief will more grievous grow.
Since none into this age was born,
But his desires were crost,
We'll take a skiff tomorrow morn,
And on wild waves be tost.

烏夜啼

黃雲城邊烏欲棲，
歸飛啞啞枝上啼。
機中織錦秦川女，
碧紗如煙隔窗語。
停梭悵然憶遠人，
獨宿空房淚如雨。

Crow's Night Song

Like clouds in twilight yellowing,
The crows flock to their nest,
On wall and tree-top chattering
Fly home to evening rest.
The maid at Ch'in Ch'uan[39] labouring,
The silk grows at the loom,
Behind the blue gauze curtain
She murmurs songs—for whom?
She stops and broods—remembering
A lover far away;
At night she lies, unchecking
Her lonely tears till day.

別董大

千里黃雲白日曛，
北風吹雁雪紛紛。
莫愁前路無知己，
天下誰人不識君。

KAO SHIH

702-765?

Parting Song

*—parting from the eldest youth of the
Tung family*

Long leagues of tawny sky shut out the day:
    On the North Wind wild geese are whirled:
      And fast, fast drives the snow.

Yet dread not loneliness upon thy way.
    What name is there in the whole world
      That thy name will not know?

杜　甫

望　嶽

岱宗夫如何，
齊魯青未了。
造化鍾神秀，
陰陽割昏曉。
盪胸生層雲，
決眥入歸鳥。
會當凌絕頂，
一覽衆山小。

TU FU[40]

712-770

Gazing at
The Great Mount[41]

To what shall I compare
The Sacred Mount that stands,
A balk of green that hath no end,
Betwixt two lands![42]
Nature[43] did fuse and blend[44]
All mystic beauty[45] there,
Where Dark and Light
Do dusk and dawn unite.[46]

Gazing, soul-cleansed, at Thee
From clouds upsprung,[47] one may
Mark with wide eyes the homing flight
Of birds. Some day
Must I thy topmost height
Mount, at one glance to see
Hills numberless
Dwindle to nothingness.

杜　甫

前出塞

挽弓當挽强，用箭當用長。

射人先射馬，擒賊先擒王。

殺人亦有限，列國自有疆。

苟能制侵陵，豈在多殺傷。

Border Campaigning

The bow you carry should be strong,
The shaft you use be long.
Aim at the rider's horse: the King
Of brigands first to justice bring.
So shall both slaughter lessened be,
And States keep their integrity.
If raid and foray you can quell,
What need for carnage fell?

贈衞八處士

人生不相見，動如參與商。
今夕復何夕，共此燈燭光。
少壯能幾時，鬢髮各已蒼。
訪舊半爲鬼，驚呼熱中腸。
焉知二十載，重上君子堂。
昔別君未婚，兒女忽成行。

Visiting an Old Friend

*—to the recluse Octavus Wei, eighth member
of the Wei family*

Unmeeting in this life we move
As stars alternate[48] rise and set.
When shall a night like this night prove,
Where thus by candle-light we're met?

How fleet is youth! Our brows now grey,
We talk of those whom we have known:
And the chafed heart moans in dismay;
For half of them are dead and gone.[49]

Unwed when you took leave of me,
Dear friend, some twenty years ago
How strange all suddenly to see
Your sons and daughters in a row!

怡然敬父執，問我來何方。

問答乃未已，兒女羅酒漿。

夜雨剪春韭，新炊間黃粱。

主稱會面難，一舉累十觴。

十觴亦不醉，感子故意長。

明日隔山嶽，世事兩茫茫。

Smiling they greet Papa's comrade
And ask about my wanderings:
Then, ere my answers all are made,
You bid them lay the table-things.

Spring leeks fresh cut in evening dew
We taste, and steaming millet mess.
"Such meetings," cries my host, "are few.
Ten flagons must we drink, no less!"

Ten flagons—Ay, but sober still.
Thanks for your faithful courtesy.
Sundered by peaks unscalable,
Tomorrow shall we strangers be.

月　夜

今夜鄜州月，閨中只獨看。

遙憐小兒女，未解憶長安。

香霧雲鬟濕，清輝玉臂寒。

何時倚虛幌，雙照淚痕乾。

Moonlight Night [50]

This night beneath the moon in yonder town[51]
I know my loved one watches all alone
(The little ones I pine for so,
Too young their father's loss to know):
Sweet mist is wet upon her cloud-like hair,
And cold the radiance on those shoulders fair.
When shall we by soft veils stand side by side,
Under one moonlight, and our tears all dried?

杜　甫

佳　人

絕代有佳人，
幽居在空谷。
自云良家子，
零落依草木。
關中昔喪亂，
兄弟遭殺戮。
官高何足論，
不得收骨肉。
世情惡衰歇，
萬事隨轉燭。
夫婿輕薄兒，
新人美如玉。

The Winsome Bride[52]

A winsome bride, surpassing fair,
  Secluded lives in a bleak glen.
    To noble name
    She can lay claim;
Yet late brought low, must needs repair
  To the wild woods, unseen of men.

Of old in the fell Border fray[53]
  Her brothers all were foully slain.
    Then titles great
    And proud estate[54]
To what avail? There as they lay,
  Their bones their kinsfolk sought in vain.

All scorn the hapless: all in life
  Like to a flickering candle blows.
    Her lord did prove
    A light-of-love:
Another maid he took to wife.
  Sweet as a lily or a rose.[55]

合昏尚知時，

鴛鴦不獨宿。

但見新人笑，

那聞舊人哭。

在山泉水清，

出山泉水濁。

侍婢賣珠迴，

牽蘿補茅屋。

摘花不插髮，

采柏動盈掬。

天寒翠袖薄，

日暮倚修竹。

The flower that shuts its leaves at night,[56]
    Though void of sense, its hour will know.
        No teal[57] upon
        The lake sleep lone.
Yet, all for his new love's delight,
    He thinks not of his old love's woe.[58]

Clear on the hills the springlet shines,
    But muddied runs adown the dale.
        Each precious stone
        That she did own
Her maids have sold: rude mountain vines
    To mend their cabin's roof they trail.

No bloom she plucks to braid her hair,
    But only sheafs of cypress[59] spray.
        In thin green sleeves
        Beneath the leaves
Of tall bamboos she lingers there,
    In winter's cold, at close of day.

杜　甫

絕句漫興九首之七

糝徑楊花鋪白氈，
點溪荷葉疊青錢。
筍根雉子無人見，
沙上鳧雛傍母眠。

Quiet Moment

Catkins tossed to left and right
Carpet all the lanes with white.
Lily-leaves on brooks are seen
Like so many coins of green.

In by the roots
Of bamboo-shoots
Young pheasants hidden keep:
And on the beach
Small ducklings, each
Beside its mother, sleep.

王　建

宮中調笑

楊柳，楊柳，日暮白沙渡口。

船頭江水茫茫，商人少婦斷腸。

腸斷，腸斷，鷓鴣夜啼失伴。

WANG CHIEN

flor. 775

To the Tune of

"Palace Laughter"

Willow-trees,
Willow-trees—
In failing sunlight by white-sanded quays.
The merchant's wife, rocked in a boat apart,
Looks on the waters' waste with aching heart.
Heart aching,
Heart aching,
The mateless partridge her night flight is making.

遊子吟

慈母手中線，遊子身上衣。

臨行密密縫，意恐遲遲歸。

誰言寸草心，報得三春暉。

Song for the Wanderer

A mother's loving fingers wove
And hemmed and sewed the coat the Wanderer wears.
In those last days
Before he went his ways,
How fine, fine were the stitches that she made!
And as she pulled each thread,
Her heart exclaimed in dread,
"How long, long must I wait till his return?"
O never say that parent's love
By children's love can be repaid.
Though every fibre of his heart should burn,
It would not dry the deep dews of her tears.[61]

節婦吟

君知妾有夫，贈妾雙明珠。

感君纏綿意，繫在紅羅襦。

妾家高樓連苑起，良人執戟明光裏。

知君用心如日月，事夫誓擬同生死。

還君明珠雙淚垂，恨不相逢未嫁時。

CHANG CHI

768-830?

The Chaste Wife's Reply [62]

On me, a wedded wife—as well you know—
A gift of rarest pearls you did bestow;
Which, grateful for your tenderness,
I pinned upon my crimson dress.
My house is tall and with fine gardens girt:
My good man is a Halberdier at Court.
Granted your love be true to the last breath—
Yet I my marriage vows must keep till death.
Sir, I return to you each precious pearl
—Yet would that I had known you as a girl!

項　斯

江村夜泊

日落江路黑，
前村人跡稀。
幾家深樹裏，
一火夜漁歸。

HSIANG SZŬ

T'ang dynasty

Mooring at Night by a Riverside Village

At sunset as the river-ways grow dark
No sign of life disturbs the gloom ahead.
    How many families
      Live there among the trees?
A single lantern shining as a spark
Lights some belated fisher home to bed.

晚　春

草木知春不久歸，
百般紅紫鬥芳菲。
楊花榆莢無才思，
惟解漫天作雪飛。

HAN YÜ[63]

768-824

Late Spring

All plants, aware that spring will soon be gone,
Their brightest rose bud purple hues put on:
    And from each emulous bloom
    Is shed a sweet perfume.

Only the willow-catkins and elm-keys,
In their simplicity, with every breeze
    Over the heavens go
    Flying like flakes of snow.

賈　島

尋隱者不遇

松下問童子，
言師採藥去。
只在此山中，
雲深不知處。

CHIA TAO[64]

777-841

The Absent Hermit

"My master's gathering herbs upon
    The hills somewhere."
(Thus from the pines a child replied)
    "I know he's gone,
But cannot tell you more: so wide
    Are the mists there."

李 紳

古 風

春種一粒粟，
秋收萬顆子。
四海無閑田，
農夫猶餓死。

鋤禾日當午，
汗滴禾下土。
誰知盤中飧，
粒粒皆辛苦。

LI SHÊN

780?-846

"Old Style"

The cob of corn in springtime sown
In autumn yields a hundredfold.
No fields are seen that fallow lie:
And yet of hunger peasants die.

As at noontide they hoe their crops,
Sweat on the grain to earth down drops.
How many tears, how many a groan,
Each morsel on thy dish did mould!

歸　鴈

瀟湘何事等閒回，

水碧沙明兩岸苔。

二十五絃彈夜月，

不勝清怨卻飛來。

CH'IEN CH'I

T'ang dynasty

Homing Wild Geese

I wondered that they ever should return
To the wild North from this sweet mere,
Where waters glimmer like pale jade
By silvery sands and mossy shade.
—And then the notes of a zither borne
Along on the moonlight played
A music infinitely sad and clear:
And their Northward flight they made.

李　賀

天上謠

天河夜轉漂迴星，銀浦流雲學水聲。
玉宮桂樹花未落，仙妾采香垂珮纓。
秦妃卷簾北窗曉，窗前植桐青鳳小。
王子吹笙鵝管長，呼龍耕煙種瑤草。
粉霞紅綬藕絲裙，青洲步拾蘭苕春。
東指羲和能走馬，海塵新生石山下。

LI HO[65]

790-816

The Starry Heavens

As in the night the Galaxy revolves
Its host of swirling stars, o'er silvery firth
Clouds with the sound of singing waters flow.
In palaces of jade blow Cassia blooms
Fadeless. There Fairy Women incense pluck
To hang in girdle sachets. Queens of eld
Raise curtains by north windows to dawn:
And near are planted Phoenix Trees[66] whereon
Green birds of Faëry rest. Princes who play
On pipes as goose-quills long do dragons call
To plough the mist for sowing magic herbs.
In skirts of lily silk with roseate cloud
Laced, in the Green Isles of the Southern Sea
They go to gather orchids all in spring.
Now pointing in the East may the Blithe Star
Speed, the floods' dust fresh rising 'neath stone hills.

白居易

驃國樂

節錄

感人在近不在遠，太平由實非由聲。

觀身理國國可濟，君如心兮民如體。

體生疾苦心憯悽，民得和平君愷悌。

貞元之民若未安，驃樂雖聞君不歡。

貞元之民苟無病，驃樂不來君亦聖。

驃樂驃樂徒喧喧，不如聞此芻蕘言。

PO CHÜ-I[67]

772-846

Outlandish Music[68]

Men's minds are swayed by near, not distant things:
Peace from reality, not rumour, springs.
Best serves the State the ruler without blame.
The Prince is as the heart, the Folk the frame.
The frame unsound, the heart must feel distress:
The Folk at peace, the Prince is in *liesse*.

Sire, should your people disaffected be,
Then where's the charm in alien minstrelsy?
Sire, should your Folk be sound, with never a strain
Of alien song, your state will still remain.
Outlandish music goes but "Rat-tat-tat":
Scorn not to listen to this homely chat.

白居易

長恨歌

漢皇重色思傾國，
御宇多年求不得。
楊家有女初長成，
養在深閨人未識。
天生麗質難自棄，
一朝選在君王側。
回眸一笑百媚生，
六宮粉黛無顏色。
春寒賜浴華清池，
溫泉水滑洗凝脂。
侍兒扶起嬌無力，
始是新承恩澤時。

The Song of Enduring Woe

A prince of Han who worshipped loveliness
Sought through his palaces long years in vain
For one whose beauty should lay kingdoms low.
A maiden of the house of Yang there was,
Fresh come to womanhood, and in the shade
Of virgin cloisters reared, unknown to men.
Too fairly formed for loneliness, one day
She stood selected for the monarch's side.
Glancing, one single smile she gave, which shed
Such radiance that through the palace halls
Each painted, pencill'd dame seemed pale and wan.

In the chill springtime she received command
To bathe in Hua-ch'ing Pool: and when the streams
Of the warm fountain laved her waxen limbs,
And softly by attendant hands upborne
She rose all faint and fair—then first it was
She gained the king's deep love and preference.

雲鬢花顏金步搖，
芙蓉帳暖度春宵。
春宵苦短日高起，
從此君王不早朝。
承歡侍宴無閒暇，
春從春遊夜專夜。
後宮佳麗三千人，
三千寵愛在一身。
金屋妝成嬌侍夜，
玉樓宴罷醉和春。
姊妹弟兄皆列土，
可憐光彩生門戶。
遂令天下父母心，
不重生男重生女。
驪宮高處入青雲，
仙樂風飄處處聞。
緩歌謾舞凝絲竹，
盡日君王看不足。

With hair like clouds she moved, and flower-like hues,
And golden plumes that nodded as she went.
Amid her curtains' roseate warmth was spent
That springtime night—the springtime night went by,
Too sadly swift; and the day mounted high.
Nor from that time was early audience held.

In feasts and merry-making day by day—
In the springtime no springtime holiday
She missed; and in the night the night was hers.
Three thousand loveliest women thronged those halls:
Three thousand loves were spared for her alone.
Golden inhabitant of Golden Bower,
Each eve, resplendently bedecked, she waited—
The banquet in Jewelled Hall being done—
Drowsy with springtime yearning as with wine.

Her sisters and her brothers all were dowered
With royal fiefs: tender benevolence
Must dignify the roof from whence she sprung.
And so a day came when, throughout the length
And breadth of all the realm, no parents wished
To bear men-children but fair daughters only.

The heights of the Li Palace soar
    Amid the azure skies;
And fairy strains, wind-blown, on every side
Are heard—soft singing and luxurious dance
    Chiming with throb of strings and wood.
    And all day long the Emperor
        Gazes unweariedly.

漁陽鞞鼓動地來，
驚破霓裳羽衣曲。
九重城闕煙塵生，
千乘萬騎西南行。
翠華搖搖行復止，
西出都門百餘里。
六軍不發無奈何，
宛轉蛾眉馬前死。
花鈿委地無人收，
翠翹金雀玉搔頭。
君王掩面救不得，
回看血淚相和流。
黃埃散漫風蕭索，
雲棧縈紆登劍閣。
峨嵋山下少人行，
旌旗無光日色薄。

—But hark, from Yü Yang thundering
   A noise of drums and cavalry
That shakes the earth and jars the melody
Of "Rainbow Robes and Coat of Gossamer"!

   Round the Imperial City gates
   Are rising clouds of flame and dust.
Ten thousand charioteers, ten thousand knights,
Race to the South-west Border; in their midst,
   Where emerald streamers flashing float,
      The Emperor's chariot rolls.
Eleven miles[70] west of the Capital
They halt—the armies will no longer march.
   There is no choice: but wistful-eyed,
   The dainty-browed beloved one
      Before the horsemen dies.

Her blosmy[71] diadem and comb of jade
And bird-wing'd golden bodkins strew the ground
Unheeded, and her plumes of feathery pearl.

And now the Emperor, who had veiled his face—
Powerless to gaze on her he could not save—
Looks back, blood mingled with his falling tears.
Where yellow sands are scattered far and wild winds
   whistling blow,
By cloudy foot-rails sinuous they mount the Sword-
   Range rim
And pass below Mount Omei where seldom travellers go:
And daily as they journey on, their standards' glint
   grows dim.

蜀江水碧蜀山青，
聖主朝朝暮暮情。
行宮見月傷心色，
夜雨聞鈴腸斷聲。
天旋地轉廻龍馭，
到此躊躇不能去。
馬嵬坡下泥土中，
不見玉顏空死處。
君臣相顧盡霑衣，
東望都門信馬歸。
歸來池苑皆依舊，
太液芙蓉未央柳。
芙蓉如面柳如眉，
對此如何不淚垂。
春風桃李花開日，
秋雨梧桐葉落時。
西宮南內多秋草，
落葉滿階紅不掃。
梨園弟子白髮新，
椒房阿監青娥老。

Fair are the rivers of Szechwan and green the Szechwan
    hills.
Morn after morn the Lord of All, eve after eve, repines.
    In exiled palace sojourning he views
          The mournful colours of the moon,
          And in the night rain hearkens to
    The agonizing sound of tinkling bells.

Heaven and the earth's upheaval being quelled,
Again returning to his native throne
The Emperor sets forth. But at one spot
His pace grows laggard, and he may not move.
There in the dust below Mount Ma-wei's slopes
He sees no trace of the earth's loveliest one,
Only the dismal scene of death. In tears
Sovereign and ministers at each other gaze;
Then dully turn their horses towards the town.
At home the lawns and lakes are as of old:
The rosy lilies yet in T'ai-yi Pool,
The willows in the gardens of Wei-yang.

Ah, but the water-lilies are her face,
The willow leaves are like her brows—he sees;
And seeing so, how can he choose but weep!
And thus, when with the winds of spring the pear
And plum trees spread their blossoms; and thus too,
When the tall forest trees[72] were bare, he mourned:
While far and wide autumnal weeds grew rank,
And fallen leaves ruddied the palace steps
Unswept. His Orchard Bands of Players now
Were white-haired all, and in the Crimson Chamber
The dark brows of the grooms were striped with age.

夕殿螢飛思悄然，
孤燈挑盡未成眠。
遲遲鐘鼓初長夜，
耿耿星河欲曙天。
鴛鴦瓦冷霜華重，
翡翠衾寒誰與共。
悠悠生死別經年，
魂魄不曾來入夢。
臨邛道士鴻都客，
能以精誠致魂魄。
爲感君王輾轉思，
遂敎方士殷勤覓。
排雲馭氣奔如電，
升天入地求之遍。
上窮碧落下黃泉，
兩處茫茫皆不見。
忽聞海上有仙山，
山在虛無縹緲間。
樓閣玲瓏五雲起，
其中綽約多仙子。
中有一人字太眞，
雪膚花貌參差是。

Nightly the fire-flies brought sad memories.
His lonely lamp he trimmed and trimmed again,
Sleepless; and slowly, slowly heard the drums
Of each long watch, until the Galaxy
With glittering lights should usher in the dawn.

Gold were the tiles above his palace roofs
(Tiles that depicted faithful matched birds)
Mantled with heavy hoar-frost flowers; and cold
Those gaudy silken coverlets unshared.
In life of death-lorn gloom, year after year,
Even her ghost came to him not in dreams.

    In Linch'iung lived a Taoist,
    One of the Hung Tu school,
Who by his special alchemy had power
To summon ghosts to flock to him at will.
    This Archimage was warranted,
    Through pity of the fretful king,
      To make a fearful quest.
Driving the clouds and mounted on the winds
      Like lightning flash he sped.
Sky-scaling and earth-probing, wide he searched
The bright empyrean and the Yellow Springs
That flow beneath the world: yet not a glimpse
On either side through endless space was seen.
At last he heard that a lone fairy isle
Far in mid-ocean lay—a single peak
Sheer in the height of the dim blue-green void;
Where glimmering towers in iridescent mist
Rose, while about in gentle numbers moved
Young fairies—one among them named "All-true",

金闕西廂叩玉扃，
轉教小玉報雙成。
聞道漢家天子使，
九華帳裏夢魂驚。
攬衣推枕起徘徊，
珠箔銀屏迤邐開。
雲髻半偏新睡覺，
花冠不整下堂來。
風吹仙袂飄飄舉，
猶似霓裳羽衣舞。
玉容寂寞淚闌干，
梨花一枝春帶雨。
含情凝睇謝君王，
一別音容兩渺茫。
昭陽殿裏恩愛絕，
蓬萊宮中日月長。
回頭下望人寰處，
不見長安見塵霧。
惟將舊物表深情，
鈿合金釵寄將去。

Of damask cheeks and skin like whitest snow.
—Passing the massy gates of gold he smote
The jewelled door that barred the western hall,
And bade the attendant elf go usher him
Into the presence of the Fairy Queen,
Who from her orient curtains hearing word
That one was come from the Han Emperor,
Startled from out of dreams, arose straightway.
Snatching a gown, her pillow thrust aside,
In haste, pell-mell, through screens of mother-o'-
        pearl
And silvery veils that opened as she passed;
With billowy hair untrimmed, still fresh from sleep,
And feathered diadem askew, she came:
And stood, her elfin sleeves wind-fanned, indeed
Like "Rainbow Robes and Coat of Gossamer",
Her woeful countenance all streaked with tears,
—A sprig of blossom drenched with springtime dew.

Then curbing her deep feeling, with fixed stare
She made obeisance to the Emperor,
And said how, since their parting, much she grieved,
His voice and shape being no longer near;
And how those days of gracious tenderness
Were ended all too soon; and in the Halls
Of Fairyland the days and months seemed long.
Turning her head she gazed below—to see
No Royal City, but a haze of dust:
Then sadly gave into his hands, as token
Of truest love, two keepsakes: a small casket,
Gaily enamelled, and a clasp of gold.

釵留一股合一扇，
釵擘黃金合分鈿。
但敎心似金鈿堅，
天上人間會相見。
臨別殷勤重寄詞，
詞中有誓兩心知。
七月七日長生殿，
夜半無人私語時。
在天願作比翼鳥，
在地願爲連理枝。
天長地久有時盡，
此恨綿綿無絕期。

"One golden prong I keep," she said, "One half
Of the enamelled casket. Look, the pin
Is broken gold, the broken casket bronze.

Bid him his mind like gold and bronze be firm,
And know that we shall meet again some time,
Whether in the sky or in the world of men."

Then parting, she enjoined him earnestly
To bear her message—and her message told
Of a deep oath that they two only knew.
—The seventh moon, upon the seventh day,
Alone at midnight in the Immortal Hall,
When none was near, in private talk they swore
In heaven as birds that yoked together fly
To fly, or else on earth to grow as trees
That twine their branches from a single stem.

"The heavens abide and earth endures," she said,
"Yet heaven and earth some time shall have an end.
But this our woe shall evermore endure."

白居易

聞哭者

昨日南鄰哭，哭聲一何苦。

云是妻哭夫，夫年二十五。

今朝北里哭，哭聲又何切。

云是母哭兒，兒年十七八。

四鄰尚如此，天下多夭折。

乃知浮世人，少得垂白髮。

余今過四十，念彼聊自悅。

從此明鏡中，不嫌頭似雪。

The Sound of Weeping

Next door somebody cried,
And all night crying kept.
A wife her husband wept:
At twenty-five he died.

In the North Lane this morn—
More weeping—and how wild!
A mother for her child
Of eighteen years did mourn.

Since all around is so—
Bereavement is so rife,
'Tis plain in this brief life
Few live white hairs to grow.

The less do I despair,
Though forty turned am I,
When in the glass I spy
A sheaf of snowy hair.

觀遊魚

遶池閑步看魚遊，
正值兒童弄釣舟。
一種愛魚心各異，
我來施食爾垂鉤。

Looking at Fishes

As all around the pool I went,
　　Watching the fishes glide:
In fishing-boat on fishing bent
　　My little ones I spied.
The love of fish did each one lead
　　As each one's fancy took him.
For I came out my fish to feed:
　　And you came out to hook him.

慵不能

架上非無書，眼慵不能看。

匣中亦有琴，手慵不能彈。

腰慵不能帶，頭慵不能冠。

午後恣情寢，午時隨事餐。

一餐終日飽，一寢至夜安。

飢寒亦閒事，況乃不飢寒。

Too Lazy

Though many a book my bookshelf graces,
I am too lazy to survey them.
I've lutes in plenty in their cases,
But rarely have a mind to play them.
I am too lazy ev'n to wear
A belt at waist, or hat on hair.

To doze at afternoon I wish—
At noon I take a casual bite,
Which makes an ample daily dish,
With sleep sufficient till the night.
Hunger and cold mean naught to me.
Besides, from both of them I'm free.

憶江南

江南好，風景舊曾諳。

日出江花紅勝火，

春來江水綠如藍。

能不憶江南。

Remembering South River Land

South River Land is a rare land,
    As from of old I know.
No flame for redness can compare
With river-blooms at daybreak there.
There waters in the springtide glow
    Deep-green like indigo.
Who can forget South River Land?

李　涉

登山

終日昏昏醉夢間，
忽聞春盡強登山。
因過竹院逢僧話，
又得浮生半日閒。

LI SHÊ

flor. 806

Talking in the Hills

How vainly all my days did seem
Wasted as in a drunken dream!
Till, seeing spring was almost gone,
I wandered up the hills alone.

There, in a bamboo-shaded walk,
With a good monk I fell to talk.
So in this tedious mortal round
One afternoon of peace I found.

憶江南

梳洗罷，獨倚望江樓。

過盡千帆皆不是，

斜暉脈脈水悠悠。

腸斷白蘋洲。

WÊN T'ING-YÜN

812?-870

To the Tune of

"Dreaming of South River Land"[74]

My dressing done,
Alone I sit to scan the tide.
A thousand sails go past the shore,
    But not the sail I am waiting for.

The slanting sun
Reddens the waters many a mile:
And still I mournfully gaze on
    Toward Whiteweed Isle.

女冠子

四月十七，正是去年今日，別君時。

忍淚佯低面，含羞半斂眉。

不知魂已斷，空有夢相隨。

除卻天邊月，沒人知。

WEI CHUANG
850?-910

To the Tune of
"Maid's Diadem"[75]

The seventeenth of the fourth moon—
    It was this day last year—
        I saw you last.
I bowed my head, but shed no tear:
    My brows were knitted fast.

My heart was broken, if you but knew!
But still in dreams I follow you.
        Except the moon
        In the far sky
    None knows of this but I.

菩薩蠻

人人盡說江南好，遊人只合江南老。

春水碧於天，畫船聽雨眠。

鑪邊人似月，皓腕凝雙雪。

未老莫還鄉，還鄉須斷腸。

WEI CHUANG

South River Land
— to the Tune of "Fair Alien Divine"

"South River Land," each traveller says,
"There is the place to end one's days".
Floating on streams' reflected skies
You hear spring rain sing lullabies.
Snowy-armed tavern-maidens there
Smile like the moon in frosty air.
But, Youth! think not of home returning:
Or sick at heart you'll die with yearning.

張　泌

寄　人

別夢依依到謝家，
小廊迴合曲闌斜。
多情只有春庭月，
猶爲離人照落花。

CHANG PI

T'ang dynasty

For Someone

In parting dream
As loth to sever
Went I to my loved one's home;
Where I did seem
Down alleys ever
Flanked with gaudy rails to roam.
But kind welcome found I none
Save of the moon, through glimmering bowers
Who for the flouted lover shone
On fallen flowers.

杜 牧

樂遊原詩

長空澹澹孤鳥沒，
萬古銷沉向此中。
看取漢家何事業，
五陵無樹起秋風。

On the City Esplanade

—whence one sees the Five Tombs of Han
Emperors

Across long skyey wastes a bird is gone.
Such is the term of countless ages past.
Where are the glories of the House of Han?
From tombs denuded mounts the autumn blast.

金谷園

繁華事散逐香塵，
流水無情草自春。
日暮東風怨啼鳥，
落花猶似墜樓人。

Golden Vale Garden

Glories of old are gone,
　　As dust made sweet
　　With print of once-beloved feet.
Pale water-weeds upon
　　The fleeting tide
　　Flaunt to the Spring their heedless pride.
Day dies: on the faint eastern gale
　　Birds mournful wail;
And flowers fall, as erst from lofty tower
　　Did Beauty's Flower.

贈別二首

一

娉娉嫋嫋十三餘，

荳蔻梢頭二月初。

春風十里揚州路，

捲上珠簾總不如。

二

多情卻似總無情，

惟覺樽前笑不成。

蠟燭有心還惜別，

替人垂淚到天明。

TU MU

A Sad Farewell

i

So light and playsome
    (Just turned thirteen)—
A sprig of mace-blossom
    In April seen!
Yet springtime winds no lovelier see
    Her curtain raising,
The length of beauty-famed city,
    From casement gazing.

ii

Who loves too much, they think
    No love to know.
Still, as farewell I drink,
    No smile I show.
The candle, as in pity of
    This sad leave-taking,
Sheds its proxy tears of love
    Until day's breaking.

落　花

高閣客竟去，小園花亂飛。

參差連曲陌，迢遞送斜暉。

腸斷未忍掃，眼穿仍欲歸。

芳心向春盡，所得是沾衣。

LI SHANG-YIN
813-858

Fallen Blossoms

My honoured guest his leave has taken;
And garden blossoms here and there
Down winding ways are blown and shaken
Out on the crimson sunset air.

Too sad to sweep their wisps away,
I gaze. No sign of him appears.
My heart spread like flower in May!
And all it earned was showers of tears.

李商隱

錦　瑟

錦瑟無端五十絃，一絃一柱思華年。
莊生曉夢迷蝴蝶，望帝春心託杜鵑。
滄海月明珠有淚，藍田日暖玉生煙。
此情可待成追憶，只是當時已惘然。

Jewelled Zither

Vain are the jewelled zither's fifty strings:
Each string, each stop, bears thought of vanished things.
The sage of his loved butterflies day-dreaming: [76]
The king that sighed his soul into a bird: [77]
Tears that are pearls, in ocean moonlight streaming: [78]
Jade mists the sun distils from Sapphire Sward: [79]
What need their memory to recall today?—
A day was theirs, which is now passed away.

李商隱

嫦　娥

雲母屏風燭影深，長河漸落曉星沉。
嫦娥應悔偷靈藥，碧海青天夜夜心。

LI SHANG-YIN

Lady of the Moon[80]

Now lamplight shades deepen on screens inlaid,
Whilst stars of morn fall with the Galaxy:
Her stolen magic draught moans the Moon-maid,
Stranded by seas of jade in yon blue sky.

自遣

得意高歌失即休，
多愁多恨亦悠悠。
今朝有酒今朝醉，
明日愁來明日愁。

A Candid Song

When all goes well, for joy I sing;
    When aught goes ill, I cease.
And, truth to tell, there's many a thing
    Might rob me of my peace.
Then drink today while drink you may.
    You ne'er may drink another day.
As for what sorrow may come to-morrow,
    Why, let it be to-morrow's sorrow!

寄　夫

夫戍邊關妾在吳，

西風吹妾妾憂夫。

一行書信千行淚，

寒到君邊衣到無。

CH'EN YÜ-LAN

T'ang dynasty

To Her Husband
at the North Frontier

While you are at the Frontier fighting
    I in the South-east dread
To feel the West Winds. Well I know
    That there they fiercer blow.

For every single line of writing
    A thousand tears I shed.
Winter is with you: are the new
    Warm clothes I sent to you?

訴衷情

永夜抛人何處去，絕來音。

香閣掩，眉斂，月將沉。

爭忍不相尋，怨孤衾。

換我心，為你心，

始知相憶深。

KU HSIUNG

Five Dynasties

Heart's Utterance

The livelong night neglecting me,
　　Where have you roamed instead?
And still no word from you is come:
　　And yet unvisited
　　Is your sweet bridal-room.
　　Waiting impatiently,
　　　　With fretted brow
　　I watch the moon decline.
　　How can I choose but rise,
Casting this hated coverlet aside,
And walk abroad to seek you far and wide?
If I could take your heart and give you mine,
　　Then you might know
　　How deep my longing is.

李　煜

清平樂

別來春半，觸目愁腸斷。

砌下落梅如雪亂，

拂了一身還滿。

雁來音信無憑，

路遙歸夢難成。

離恨恰如春草，

更行更遠還生。

LI YÜ[81]

937-978

To the Tune of
"Light Flowing Music"

To one who lonely sees the springtime close,
Each thing that strikes the eye bids the heart break,
Plum-blossoms tumbling as dishevelled snows
  Down over steps of stone, 'tis vain
   From off one's dress to shake:
As soon as shaken off, they cling again.

   See, the wild geese are come,
   But voice, but word, is dumb.[82]
So long a road no wistful dream may take.
   Farewell's sorrowing
   Is like grass in spring:
   How far so e'er you go,
   Yet faster will it grow.

李　煜

虞美人

春花秋月何時了，往事知多少。

小樓昨夜又東風，故國不堪回首月明中。

雕闌玉砌應猶在，只是朱顏改。

問君能有幾多愁，恰似一江春水向東流。

To the Tune of

"Fair Lady Yü"

When shall the spring's last blossom, when shall autumn's
    last moon fail?
        Who knows the term of mortal days?
On the watch-tower last night there blew westward a
    springtime gale:
But to my native realm by moonlight dared I not bend
    my gaze.

Are those flower-wreathed balconies, those halls of jade
    as of yore?
        Yes: only waned is beauty's rose.
Tell me how many grievances are yet for thee in store?
No fewer than spring-rash waters rush as the eastward
    River flows.

李 煜

相見歡

無言獨上西樓，

月如鉤，

寂寞梧桐深院鎖清秋。

剪不斷，

理還亂，

是離愁，

別是一般滋味在心頭。

Up the Western Stair

— to the Tune of "Joy at Meeting"

Alone and silent up the Western Stair.
    A sickle moon hangs there:
    And in the court below
One lonely tree is lapped in the cold autumn air.

Shearing will not sever—no,
Nor sorting disentwine their woe,
    When lovers part.
Sure 'tis a special savour in the heart.

浣溪紗

一曲新詞酒一杯，
去年天氣舊亭臺，
夕陽西下幾時回。
無可奈何花落去，
似曾相識燕歸來，
小園香徑獨徘徊。

YEN SHU[83]

991-1055, Northern Sung dynasty

Mutability

A new song, and another cup of wine!
An air of yesteryear is haunting still
This ancient lodge. But will that twilight day
That's sinking in the West come back again?

And ineluctably the blossoms fall.
And swallows, like the ones I knew, return.
And mournfully I tread the scented ways
Of this small pleasure-garden, to and fro.

陶　者

陶盡門前土，屋上無片瓦。
十指不沾泥，鱗鱗居大廈。

MEI YAU-CH'ÊN

1022-1060

The Tile-maker

The clay about his house is dug away
To make his tiles, whose roof of tiles is bare;
That they whose hands were never wet with clay
May keep their palaces in good repair.

畫眉鳥

百囀千聲隨意移，
山花紅紫樹高低。
始知鎖向金籠聽，
不及林間自在啼。

OU-YANG HSIU[84]

1007-1072

The Hua-mei's Song

Warbling the million silver trills
    That with her mood may go,
In trees abloom on scented hills
    She moves now high now low.

And as I listen, now I see
    That locked in cage of gold
Never as in the woodlands free
    So sweet a tale she told.

采桑子

畫船載酒西湖好，

急管繁絃，

玉盞催傳，

穩泛平波任醉眠。

行雲却在行舟下，

空水澄鮮，

俯仰留連，

疑是湖中別有天。

OU-YANG HSIU

Sweet is the Western Lake

— to the Tune of "Mulberry-pickers"

In painted sloop if wine you take,
   Sweet is the Western Lake:
      As wood and string
      Go ding-a-ding:
   And fast the glittering glass
   From hand to hand you pass;
Soft gliding over halcyon seas
Alert or drowsy as you please.
    See—wisps of cloud afloat
    Beneath the floating boat;
      Where flood and air
      Show limpid fair
A moment as you linger there.
You'd fancy in the waters deep
   Another heaven did sleep.

杜小山

寒夜

寒夜客來茶當酒，
竹爐湯沸火初紅。
尋常一樣窗前月，
纔有梅花便不同。

TU HSIAO-SHAN

Sung dynasty

Makeshift Entertainment

A cold night for a guest, I fear:
And tea must serve for wine.
The water boils, and the dim room
Is reddened with fire-light.
In at the window moonbeams peer—
But see, in the moonshine,
A shadowy plum-tree spray has come
To beautify the night.

蘇　軾

水調歌頭

明月幾時有，把酒問青天。
不知天上宮闕，今夕是何年。
我欲乘風歸去，惟恐瓊樓玉宇
高處不勝寒。起舞弄清影，
何似在人間。

Remembrance in Mid-Autumn

— to the Tune of "Barcarole Prelude"

"When did this glorious moon begin to be?"
Cup in hand, I asked of the azure sky:
And wondered in the palaces of the air
What calendar this night do they go by.
Yes, I would wish to mount the winds and wander there
At home; but dread those onyx towers and halls of jade
Set so immeasurably cold and high.
To tread a measure, to sport with fleshless shade,
How alien to our frail mortality!

轉朱閣，低綺戶，

照無眠。不應有恨，

何事長向別時圓。人有悲歡離合，

月有陰晴圓缺，此事古難全。

但願人長久，千里共嬋娟。

Her light round scarlet pavilion, 'neath broidered screen, down streams
> On me that sleepless lie.
> Ah, vain indeed is my complaining:

But why must she beam at the full on those that sundered sigh?

As men have their weal and woe, their parting and meeting, it seems

The moon has her dark and light, her phases of fulness and waning.
> Never is seen perfection in things that die.
> Yet would I crave one solitary boon:
> Long be we linked with light of the fair moon
> Over large leagues of distance, thou and I.

蘇　軾

書鄢陵王主簿所畫折枝

瘦竹如幽人，幽花如處女。

低昂枝上雀，搖蕩花間雨。

雙翎決將起，衆葉紛自舉。

可憐採花蜂，清蜜寄兩股。

若人富天巧，春色入毫楮。

懸知君能詩，寄聲求妙語。

Written on a Painting of Flowers Done by Intendant Wang of Yen-ling

Slim bamboos like hermits frail:
Flowerets dim as virgins pale.
Bird upon the sprig a-swaying,
Raindrops faint on petals playing.

Feathery pinions poised for flight;
Leaves all trembling toward the light.
Bees, sweet robbers, blossoms nigh;
Deep in nectar to the thigh.

He that could stencil
Such lovely work,
I know in his pencil
Does springtime lurk.

In penning this
It is my design
From him to elicit
Some verse divine.

蘇　軾

飲湖上初晴後雨

水光瀲灩晴方好，
山色空濛雨亦奇。
欲把西湖比西子，
淡妝濃抹總相宜。

The Western Lake
When Rain is Falling[86]

These pools, so lovely when their bright
Wavelets are glancing in sunlight,
Still, when the hills are dimmed with rain,
Their pristine loveliness retain.
For symbol of the Western Lake
The Western Maid you well may take,
Whether adorned with white and rose
Or in unpainted grace she goes.

吉祥寺賞牡丹

人老簪花不自羞，
花應羞上老人頭。
醉歸扶路人應笑，
十里珠簾半上鈎。

Admiring Peony-blossoms at the Monastery of Good Omens

Though old, no shame it is to me
    With flowers to be bedizened.
Nay, flowers should rather shame to be
    Stuck on a pate so wizened.
Nor do I much resent men's smiles
    As, groping tipsily,
I teeter home—and for three miles
    Each lifted curtain see.

蘇　軾

贈劉景文

荷盡已無擎雨蓋，
菊殘猶有傲霜枝。
一年好景君須記，
最是橙黃橘綠時。

Winter

Now water-lily plants are dead,
Their wan umbrellas all are lost.
A few chrysanthemums have stayed
On withered stems to brave the frost.
All through the year, I still will hold,
No finer sight is to be seen
Than when sweet oranges turn gold
While yet the mandarines are green.

清平樂

春歸何處，寂寞無行路。

若有人知春去處，

喚取歸來同住。

春無踪跡誰知，

除非問取黃鸝。

百囀無人能解，

因風吹過薔薇。

HUANG T'ING-CHIEN

1045-1105

To the Tune of

"Light Flowing Music"

Whither is Springtime gone—
Alone along lone ways?
If you should know where now she strays,
Bid her come back and linger on.

But no, no sign of her!—unless
Her news the oriole discloses
In notes whose sound is meaningless,
Blown by the wind over sweet roses.

漁家傲

天接雲濤連曉霧，
星河欲轉千帆舞。
彷彿夢魂歸帝所。
聞天語，
殷勤問我歸何處。
我報路長嗟日暮，
學詩謾有驚人句。
九萬里風鵬正舉。
風休住，
蓬舟吹取三山去。

A Dream

Where in the heavens that mingle billowy clouds and
    mists of morn
On the River of Stars awhirl go a-flutter a thousand
    sails,
Even as one in a dream home-coming to God's abode,
        I heard Heaven speak,
    Softly inquiring whither was I bound.

I answered: "Long is the way; Ay me, and the day fails:
And for all my love of Poesy scarce a stirring line have
    I found.
O'er winds of myriad leagues the Roc into flight would
    break.
        Winds, be not slowed
    Till to the hills of Faëry my bark be borne!"

李清照

如夢令

昨夜雨疏風驟，
濃睡不消殘酒。
試問捲簾人，
卻道海棠依舊。
知否，知否，
應是綠肥紅瘦。

LI CH'ING-CHAO

Madrigal:
"As in a Dream"

Last night in the light rain as rough winds blew,
My drunken sleep left me no merrier.
I question one that raised the curtain, who
Replies: "The wild quince trees—are as they were."
        But no, but no!
Their rose is waning, and their green leaves grow.

李清照

聲聲慢

尋尋覓覓，
冷冷清清，
悽悽慘慘戚戚。
乍暖還寒時候，
最難將息。
三杯兩盞淡酒，
怎敵他，
晚來風急。

LI CH'ING-CHAO

Sorrow

I pine and peak
And questless seek
Groping and moping to linger and languish
Anon to wander and wonder, glare, stare and start
     Flesh chill'd
     Ghost thrilled
     With grim dart
And keen canker of rankling anguish.

Sudden a gleam
Of fair weather felt
But fled as fast—and the ice-cold season stays.
How hard to have these days
In rest or respite, peace or truce.
Sip upon sip of tasteless wine
Is of slight use
To counter or quell
The fierce lash of the evening blast.

雁過也，

正傷心，

却是舊時相識。

滿地黃花堆積，

憔悴損，

如今有誰堪摘。

守着窗兒，

獨自怎生得黑。

梧桐更兼細雨，

到黃昏，

點點滴滴。

這次第，

怎一個，

愁字了得。

The wild geese—see—
Fly overhead
Ah, there's the grief
That's chief—grief beyond bearing,
Wild fowl far faring
In days of old you sped
Bearing my true love's tender thoughts to me.
Lo, how my lawn is rife with golden blooms
Of bunched chrysanthemums—
Weary their heads they bow.
Who cares to pluck them now?
While I the casement keep
Lone, waiting, waiting for night
    And, as the shades fall
Upon broad leaves,[88] sparse rain-drops drip.
    Ah, such a plight
Of grief—grief unbearable, unthinkable.

宴山亭

北行見杏花作

裁翦冰綃，輕叠數重，

冷淡胭脂勻注。

新樣靚妝，豔溢香融，

羞殺蘂珠宮女。

易得凋零，

更多少，無情風雨。

愁苦。

問院落淒涼，

幾番春暮。

CHAO CHI

Sung dynasty

On Seeing an
Almond-tree in Blossom

(The Emperor addresses the blossoms)[89]

Filigree of silken fleece
Shorn from thinnest shreds of ice;
Flake on flake so lightly placed,
With chill tints of colour laced;
> Fresh and fair
> Beyond compare;
Fragrant, delicate, winsome thing!
Fairy-women who, they tell,
In the Pearl-Bloom Palace dwell,
When they hear men speak your name,
Hide their heavenly heads for shame.
Fain, too fain, to fade away!
Soon will come that baneful day
When with boisterous winds and rain
All your beauty shall be slain.
> Ah, well-a-day!
> Come tell me, pray,
How many and many a springtime evening
> Has come and gone
> Since, bleak and lone,
My ravaged royal halls lie mouldering!

憑寄離恨重重，

這雙燕何曾，會人言語。

天遙地遠，萬水千山，

知他故宮何處。

怎不思量，

除夢裏有時曾去。

無據，

和夢也新來不做。

(He addresses the swallows)

  O Messenger of springtime, follow
  The winds of spring and bear
My tale of woe and pain, of pain and woe.
   —But never, never swallow
  Did human language know.
And such a world of distance lies between:
  Wide lakes and rivers green
And mountains manifold and plains of dust.[90]
And where that palace is how can you say?
Each road to it I measure night and day.
    Only in dreams
  I sometimes visit there.
    But dreams, meseems,
    Are not to trust:
  Of late such dreams are rare.

朱敦儒

漁父詞
好事近

搖首出紅塵，
醒醉更無時節。
活計綠簑青笠，
慣披霜衝雪。
晚來風定釣絲閑，
上下是新月。
千里水天一色，
看孤鴻明滅。

CHU TUN-JU

?1080-1175, Southern Sung dynasty

Angler's Song

—to the Tune of "With Much Ado"

Well, here's a long good-bye to Vanity Fair.
    Henceforth, drunk or sober, never
    With time to grapple shall I endeavour.
In dull-green fisher's cloak of leaves I'll go,
    With bright-green bonnet of woven reeds:
    These shall be all my earthly needs;
    And welcome frost and the icy air
      And buffeting of snow!

Now of an evening when the winds are whist,
    And idle hangs my line:
    Above a moon and a moon below;
    And seas and heaven in one great glow:
    I'll watch the grey geese as they twine
      From light into the mist.

楊萬里

初二日苦熱

人言長江無六月，我言六月無長江。

只今五月已如許，六月更來何可當。

船艙周圍各五尺，且道此中底寬窄。

上下東西與南北，一面是水五面日。

日光煮水復成湯，此外何處能清涼。

掀篷更無風半點，揮扇只有汗如漿。

吾曹避暑自無處，飛蠅投吾求避暑。

吾不解飛且此住，飛蠅解飛不飛去。

YANG WAN-LI

1124-1206

Sweltering in July

Men say there's no July on the Blue River:
    I say there's no Blue River in July.
Ev'n as it is, July is worse than ever.
    O what a prospect as the days go by!

This cabin (five foot round—it might be wider!)
    As cabins go, is yet an ample one.
Above, below, North, South, East, West—consider:
    One side is water, and the rest is sun!

The water fast its boiling point is nearing.
    Where, where can one find shelter from those beams?
One lifts the awning—not a breath is stirring.
    One plies a fan—and sweat falls down in streams.

We from the heat lack all alleviations.
    The flies that swarm on us some refuge find.
We cannot fly, and suffer on with patience:
    Those flies that can, to fly are not inclined.

四時田園雜興
一首

晝出耘田夜績麻，
村莊兒女各當家。
童孫未解供耕織，
也傍桑陰學種瓜。

Country Life

At noon to hoe
Their crops they go;
At night they spin indoors:
No lad or lass
But can surpass
In skill at country chores.

Those babes as yet
Too small to set
At spinning or at sowing,
Shaded by leaves
Of mulberry-trees,
Practise cucumber-growing.

龍挂

成都六月天大風，發屋動地聲勢雄。

黑雲崔嵬行風中，凜如鬼神塞虛空。

霹靂迸火射地紅，上帝有命起伏龍。

龍尾不捲曳天東，壯哉雨點車軸同。

山摧江溢路不通，連根拔出千尺松。

未言爲人作年豐，偉觀一洗芥蔕胸。

LU YU[92]

1125-1210

A Portent

When the great wind in the sixth moon o'erwhelmed
The skies at Ch'eng-tu, lifting houses whole,
Shaking the land with fearful din, black clouds
Of craggy shale were borne in the wind's midst:
A ghostly dankness covered the wide air;
And lightnings shot red fire down on earth.
The Lord of Heaven bade lurking dragons rise,
Which trailed their half-furled standards from the east.
Great rain-drops clattered, large as axle-trees:
Mountains o'er-toppled: and the river floods
All passage barred; and by their roots uprent
Were pine-trees furlongs tall. None knows as yet
If plenteous year be augured. Yet this sight
Stupendous cleansed the heart of vulgar cares.

陸　游

秋夜將曉出籬門迎涼有感

三萬里河東入海，
五千仞嶽上摩天。
遺民淚盡胡塵裏，
南望王師又一年。

LU YU

Reproach

*—on the indifference of the Southern Sung Court to
the plight of their fellow-countrymen in the North,
still under the domination of the Juchen Tartars*

Seaward a myriad leagues is pouring
    The Yellow River's stream:
Mountains five thousand fathoms soaring
    One with the Heavens seem.

Our folk, with Tartar grime beset,
    Tears drained from every eye,
Look to the South for aid. And yet
    Another year goes by.

示　兒

死去元知萬事空，
但悲不見九州同。
王師北定中原日，
家祭無忘告乃翁。

LU YU

Testament to His Son

With death although
Right well I know
All things are done;
Yet woe were me
Never to see
This Realm at one.

Whatever day
Our armies may
The North unite,
That news mind well
Your sire to tell
In sacred rite.[93]

辛棄疾

西江月

醉裏且貪歡笑，要愁那得工夫。
近來始覺古人書，信著全無是處。

昨夜松邊醉倒，問松我醉何如。
只疑松動要來扶，以手推松曰去。

A Truce to Sorrow

There's comfort, anyhow, in drink—
    And time enough for grieving.
Our sages are (of late I think)
    Not always worth believing.

Dead drunk, I said to the pine-tree,
    "Tell me, am I far gone?"
And as he bent to succour me,
    I sighed to him—"Move on!"

醜奴兒

書博山道中壁

少年不識愁滋味，
愛上層樓，愛上層樓，
爲賦新詞强説愁。
而今識盡愁滋味，
欲説還休，欲説還休，
却道天涼好個秋。

Enlightenment

In youth, ere Grief to me was known
I loved to climb on high, I loved to climb on high:
    In many a laboured lay
    Grief would I there portray.

But now, with Grief familiar grown,
Slower to speak am I, slower to speak am I.
    At most, I pause and say,
    "What a fine autumn day!"

辛棄疾

清平樂
獨宿博山王氏庵

遶牀饑鼠，

蝙蝠翻燈舞。

屋上松風吹急雨，

破紙窗間自語。

平生塞北江南，

歸來華髮蒼顏。

布被秋宵夢覺，

眼前萬里江山。

HSIN CH'I-CHI

In Exile

Around my bed crawl hungry rats; bats round the lamp
flit to and fro.
Pine-forest winds through the torn roof blow
gusts of rain.
Slat-slatting goes my tattered paper window-
pane.

A long life North and South wandering, weary and
silver-haired, I go.
This autumn night, wrapped in thin plaid, from
sorriest dreams
Waking, I sigh for our ancestral hills and streams.

村　晚

草滿池塘水滿陂，
山銜落日浸寒漪。
牧童歸去橫牛背，
短笛無腔信口吹。

LEI CHEN

Sung dynasty

Evening in a Village

On ponds with grasses cluttered and on rills
    bespangled all with gold
    the sunlight, tinged with cold,
        fades, while the sun sets beyond
        far-off hills.

Astride his buffalo a shepherd boy
    homeward is idly straying
    and on his short pipe playing,
        notes out of time and tune, and laughs
        for joy.

文天祥

正氣歌 並序

余囚北庭，坐一土室。室廣八尺，深可四尋，單扉
低小，白間短窄，汙下而幽暗。當此夏日，諸氣萃
然。雨潦四集，浮動牀几，時則爲水氣。塗泥半朝，
蒸漚歷瀾，時則爲土氣。乍晴暴熱，風道四塞，時
則爲日氣。簷陰薪爨，助長炎虐，時則爲火氣。倉
腐寄頓，陳陳逼人，時則爲米氣。駢肩雜遝，腥臊
汙垢，時則爲人氣。或圊溷浮屍，或腐鼠雜出，時
則爲穢氣。疊是數氣，當之者鮮不爲厲。而予以孱

WEN T'IEN-HSIANG[95]

1236-1282

Song of Honour

*—written in prison in
1281, with a preface in prose*

PREFACE

Captive in the Mongolian capital, I lie in an earthen chamber, eight cubits wide, five fathoms deep, with a foul low floor and murky. The season being summer, all manner of exhalations are here united. Puddles of rain water are all about, making bed and table insecure: and thus is formed the Exhalation of Water. From half-sodden clay there reeks the effluvium of stable mire: and this makes the Exhalation of Earth. In sudden bursts of sultry weather, each breath of wind is stifled: and this makes the Exhalation of the Sun. Faggots cooking under dark eaves augment the torment of heat: and this makes the Exhalation of Fire. Accumulated rotting stores assail the sense with incessant odour: and this makes the Exhalation of Grain. Convicts huddled shoulder to shoulder are squalid and rank with noisome stench: and this makes the Exhalation of Man. Then privies, and mangled corpses, and carrion rats, contribute their fetor: and this makes the Exhalation of Defilement. Which various exhalations being joined together, few are their sustainers that are not impaired.

弱俯仰其間，於玆二年矣，幸而無恙，是殆有養致然。然亦安知所養何哉。孟子曰：我善養吾浩然之氣。彼氣有七，吾氣有一。以一敵七，吾何患焉。況浩然者，乃天地之正氣也。作正氣歌一首。

Yet I, weak though I be and feeble, sojourning amidst them these two years, remain unscathed: which, methinks, must argue a right special discipline or moral preparation. Would you know in what this discipline consists? Mencius has said: "I foster in myself the Spirit of Nobility". Seven Exhalations to my One. One holding his own against seven, what cause have I to complain? Nay, the less so, as this Nobility is nothing else than the Breath of Truth which pervades the Heavens and the Earth. Herewith I make this *Song of the Breath of Truth*.

天地有正氣，雜然賦流形。

下則爲河嶽，上則爲日星。

於人曰浩然，沛乎塞蒼冥。

皇路當清夷，含和吐明庭。

時窮節乃見，一一垂丹青。

在齊太史簡，在晉董狐筆。

在秦張良椎，在漢蘇武節。

爲嚴將軍頭，爲嵇侍中血。

爲張睢陽齒，爲顏常山舌。

或爲遼東帽，清操厲冰雪。

或爲出師表，鬼神泣壯烈。

或爲渡江楫，慷慨吞胡羯。

或爲擊賊笏，逆豎頭破裂。

是氣所磅礡，凜烈萬古存。

當其貫日月，生死安足論。

POEM

Set between Heaven and Earth, the breath of Truth
Diversely into divers forms is given.
Beneath, the hills it makes and rivers both:
Above, it moulds the sun and stars of heaven;
And among men, being named Nobility,
Wells and o'erwhelms the world's infinitude.
When Governance proceeds in equity,
Mildly it shows itself in gentle mood:
In time of woe, it blazons Loyalty's name
To shine eternally in Halls of Fame.
Witness those faithful chroniclers of yore
Who doomed themselves to die that truth might stand;
Witness the iron mace the hireling bore;
The signet clasped in a far alien land;
Those captains who would only headless yield;
The life-blood spattered on a liege's gown;
Or he that gnashed at rebels in the field;
Or he that, tongueless, treachery yet cried down,
And one who would into mean exile go,
His loyalty more pure than ice or snow.
Then one there was, that wise War-Counsellor,
Made angels weep to mark his hardihood;
And one who in mid-river splashed his oar,
Pledging his valour against Tartar blood;
Another that, with righteous anger fired,
With ivory tablet pashed the recreant's crown.
This was the Spirit which these men inspired
To deeds whose praises never shall be done.
Seeing both sun and moon it may surmount,
Both life and death it holds of small account.

地維賴以立，天柱賴以尊。

三綱實繫命，道義爲之根。

嗟予遘陽九，隸也實不力。

楚囚纓其冠，傳車送窮北。

鼎鑊甘如飴，求之不可得。

陰房闃鬼火，春院閟天黑。

牛驥同一皂，雞棲鳳凰食。

一朝濛霧露，分作溝中瘠。

如此再寒暑，百沴自辟易。

哀哉沮洳場，爲我安樂國。

豈有他繆巧，陰陽不能賊。

顧此耿耿在，仰視浮雲白。

悠悠我心悲，蒼天曷有極。

哲人日已遠，典型在夙昔。

風簷展書讀，古道照顏色。

On this the hinges of the earth are founded:
The pillars of heav'n from this their honour share.
All loyalties by its decrees are bounded:
Justice and Righteousness are rooted there.
Alas, that I, fallen upon evil days,
My service proven of but feeble worth
In dress of durance, máde a common gaze,
Am dragged on hurdle to the farthest North.
In cauldron seethed would I gladly be;
But such deliv'rance is not granted me.
In this sad cell, where will-o'-the-wisps glow pale
Darkened is all the springtime's loveliness.
Where ox and courser crowd at common stall,
The Phoenix with the farmyard fowl must mess.
Waiting that day when foul airs infested,
Cast in a kennel, a grim corpse I be,
Two winters long, with countless ills molested,
I have held the course, and gained the mastery.
I swear, in my rank dungeon's dear despite,
I count it as a garden of delight.
Whence comes such wondrous cunning else, to be
A power Time's ravages may not defeat?
It is this steadfast Spirit dwells in me.
Raising my head, I watch the white clouds fleet.
Long have I pondered, brooding as in dream:
When shall the vast of Heaven see all ended?
Lovers of wisdom, farther though they seem,
Yet have they left to us their Vision Splendid.
By draughty eaves, I spread my book and read:
The Ancient Way shines to me in my need.

漁父曲

雨過暮雲收，江空涼日出。

輕簑獨釣翁，一曲秋風笛。

宿鷺忽驚飛，點破煙波碧。

YEH YUNG

Yüan dynasty

Fisherman's Ditty

After the rain in the cool of day
When every cloud has been swept away,
On the vacant river the sun shines out;
And you see in his reed shawl wrapped about
      An aged angler stray.
"The Autumn Wind" on his flute he plays;
And a crouching heron the noise dismays
Starts from the sedge. As his flight he takes
The misty waters' jade-green breaks
      In a shower of silver spray.

詠梅花

終日尋春不見春，
芒鞋踏破嶺頭雲。
歸來笑撚梅花嗅，
春在枝頭已十分。

"PLUM-BLOSSOM SISTER", A BUDDHIST NUN

Yüan dynasty

A Song of Plum-blossom

I sought for springtime all the day,
But springtime seemed to shun my way;
And wore my woven sandals bare,
Walking through misty mountain air;
And then at last, when I came home,
Toyed with a sprig of plum-blossom.
Smelling its sweet, I smiled for pleasure;
For here was springtime in full measure.

送陳秀才還沙上省墓

滿衣血淚與塵埃，
亂後還鄉亦可哀。
風雨梨花寒食過，
幾家墳上子孫來。

KAO CH'I

1336-1374

War Tombs[96]

Dress begrimed with dust and tears and gore,
Sad is homecoming after years of war.[97]
Pear-blooms storm-swept, the Tomb Feast Eve being
    done,
How many youthful mourners by graves moan!

飲　酒

儒生好奇古，出口談唐虞。

倘生羲皇前，所談竟何如。

古人既已死，古道存遺書。

一語不能踐，萬卷徒空虛。

我願但飲酒，不復知其餘。

君看醉鄉人，乃在天地初。

LIN HUNG

Ming dynasty

On Wine

Confucianists that love old ways
    Forever prate of ancient glories.[98]
Where, if they lived in ancient days,
    Should they find matter for their stories?

Since all the ancients long are dead,
    And all their lore consigned to paper;
And out of date is all they've said:
    Then all their wisdom is but vapour.[99]

For me, I find my inspiration
    In wine: the rest I do not mind.
Yet, mark you, in inebriation
    The truly primitive you'll find.[100]

錢秉鐙

效淵明飲酒

寄生大塊中，何者爲我故。

譬如逆旅物，暫有安足據。

在世雖百年，畢竟舍之去。

臨行豈不戀，戀亦不得住。

所以達觀人，澹然隨所遇。

委順生死間，不厭亦不慕。

日飲一杯酒，可以全此趣。

CH'IEN PING-TÊNG

Ming dynasty

On Wine,
*   After Yüan-ming* [101]

In our abode beneath the sky
    Nought stable may we trace.
'Tis as a caravanserai
    Where we may halt a space.
Though you should live a hundred year,
    At length you must away:
Nor yet without a wistful tear;
    Yet tears can gain no stay.
Therefore it is that men of sense,
    Taking what life may bring,
Leave times and tides to Providence,
    —Unmoved, unmurmuring.
A daily cup of wine, you'll find,
    Fosters this pleasant state of mind.

凱　歌

銜枚夜度五千兵，
密領軍符號令明。
狹巷短兵相接處，
殺人如草不聞聲。

SHÊN MING-CH'ÊN

Ming dynasty

Paean[102]

Five thousand fighting men
    Go noiseless in the night.
Close Order they maintain:
    They march with lips sealed tight.[103]

In narrow street and lane
    With small arms instantly
They strike: and swaths of slain
    Like grass, fall silently.

長相思

山一程，水一程，身向榆關那畔行，
夜深千帳鐙。

風一更，雪一更，聒碎鄉心夢不成，
故園無此聲。

NALAN HSINGTEH[104]

?1655-1685, Ch'ing dynasty

To the Tune of

"Love-longing"

By weary turn
Of river and bourn
On unto Elm Pass yonder must I go,
Where through the dark a thousand tent-lights glow.
The long night-watches round,
In roar of wind and snow
Dreams that would wander homeward all are drowned.
—At home is no such sound.

沁園春

瞬息浮生，薄命如斯，
低徊怎忘。
記繡榻閒時，並吹紅雨，
雕闌曲處，同倚斜陽。
夢好難留，詩殘莫續，
贏得更深哭一場。
遺容在，只靈颸一轉，
未許端詳。

NALAN HSINGTEH

To His Lost Bride

—to the Tune of "Springtime in Provincial Garden"[105]

Mortal sojourning short-dated,
Tender breath of life ill-fated!
How can I but brood and fret?
    How can I forget?
Yet I mind me how we played
When your work aside you laid,
Played at blowing showers of roses
By your frame of stretched brocade;
Or together at a bend
Of the quaint-carved balustrade
    In sunset we leaned.
Fairest dreams must soonest fade:
Broken measures are not mended.
    All is ended:
Only in the small hours may I weep and weep my fill.
    Your image sweet is with me still:
Ah, but your sprite has veered away
    Nor ever may
Linger with mine as evening closes.

重尋碧落茫茫，

料短髮朝來定有霜。

便人間天上，塵緣未斷，

春花秋月，觸緒還傷。

欲結綢繆，翻驚搖落，

兩處鴛鴦各自涼。

眞無奈，把聲聲簷雨，

譜出回腸。

Away now and away down in some skyey jewelled dell—
Tell me, was your thin hair silvered with frost this morn?
    Though I on earth and you in heaven dwell,
        Yet is our earthly bond unshorn:
        For every springtime flower that blows
        (Yea, and all autumn moons that shine)
        Wrenching the soul, renews our woes.
        Aye, but our lives to re-entwine—
           At such a great assay
           We tremble in dismay,
Two sundered loving mated birds that each for other
    pine.
           Woe is me, woe again
        Hearing that sound, the sound of rain
          Under the eaves, its score
        Wearing and wringing the heart's core.

憶江南

宿雙林禪院有感

心灰盡，有髮未全僧。

風雨消磨生死別，

似曾相識只孤檠。

情在不能醒。

搖落後，清吹那堪聽。

淅瀝暗飄金井葉，

乍聞風定又鐘聲。

薄福薦傾城。

NALAN HSINGTEH

Written while Staying at Double-Grove Monastery

—to the Tune of "Remembering South River Land"

Embers of my heart are dead—
Bonze as yet untonsured.
With wind and rain all trace is worn
Of sorrows out of parting born.
       Yet this lone lamp to me
       Remains familiar still:
       Still burns unquenchable.

Beauty faded, who can bear
       To hear fresh breezes blown?
Faint upon the sleety air
Flutter leaves by Golden Well.
       As sudden the wind's moan
Dies, there sounds a tinkling bell.
       Then does the hapless one
Mourn the fairest of the fair.

蝶戀花

又到綠楊曾折處，
不語垂鞭，
踏遍清秋路。
衰草連天無意緒，
雁聲遠向蕭關去。
不恨天涯行役苦，
只恨西風，
吹夢成今古。
明日客程還幾許，
霑衣況是新寒雨。

NALAN HSINGTEH

"Blossoms Loved by Butterflies"

Here where we parted and did break
Green poplar sprigs that each should take
    For true love's sake,
—Wordless, riding-crop limp trailing,
Again those well-remembered ways
I tread, in the clear autumn rays;
Fronting a world of blear grass, feeling failing:
And far unto the Frontier Pass wild geese are wailing.

'Tis not the bitterness of ever wending
    On pilgrimage unending:
No, 'tis the West Wind's moaning makes me
    sorrow,
    Which all our dreams must blow
Into the nothingness of Evermore.
Yet farther, ever farther, on the morrow
    The wanderer must go,
    Dress drenched, afresh to face wet winter frore.

栽樹自嘲

七十猶種樹，
旁人莫笑癡。
古來雖有死，
好在不先知。

YÜAN MEI

1715-1797

Self-banter
on Arboriculture

Still planting trees at seventy!
　　Yet mock not, neighbour,
　　My wasted labour.
　　Yes, mortal men
　　Must die. But when?
　　Fortunately
　　None can foresee.

論　詩

李杜詩篇萬口傳，

至今已覺不新鮮。

江山代有才人出，

各領風騷數百年。

CHAO I

1726-1814

On Poems

Songs of Li Po and Tu Fu,
    Once all the rage,
Now seem scarcely suited to
    Our modern age.

Each generation can its Genius show:
They honour him—a hundred years or so.

七里瀨

煙江漁互唱，
小艇人相語。
峯迴不見峯，
路轉疑無路。
遙見山下人，
漸入山中去。

LI TIAO-YÜAN

flor. 1763

Seven-mile Shallows

Fishers yodelling on the misty river
    One to another from their dinghies call.
Tall peaks recede; and our course is ever
    Veering into no course at all.
        Yonder you may
        View faraway
Blue hills with shapes of men below;
        Whom momently
        Through clouds you'll see
Into the mountain dimness go.

Notes

1. The first four poems in this anthology are from the *Book of Poetry*, an ancient collection of practically anonymous songs which date from about the 12th century to the 6th century B.C.
2. Some scholars suggest that "sea-hawks" is not as accurate as "ospreys" for 關雎. Turner may be refurbishing the more archaic word (see *O.E.D.* under "sea-hawk"), but the objection remains about the incongruous associations of the predatory sea-hawk with a "Courtship Song". (*Ed.*)
3. Floating Hearts: "The Floating Heart Lily" has leaves which resemble those of the buckbean, popularly called "Floating Hearts" in the U.S.A.
4. In this translation metre and rhyming attempt to approximate the original.
5. Fern is substituted for "brocken".
6. Attributed to Confucius (551-479 B.C.). Metre and rhyming attempt to approximate the original. The Chinese title literally means "Alas for the *Eupatorium Sinensis*: A Song of Resignation". The plant referred to, a kind of boneset, is aromatic and symbolized nobleness and royalty.
   The story goes that Confucius, having vainly offered his services to various princes, as he returned to his own country, was moved by the sight of this "royal" plant growing unnoticed in a secluded valley, and sang the song to the music of his lute.
7. Liu Ch'ê, commonly referred to as Han Wu-ti ("the Warrior Emperor"), was the most illustrious ruler of his line. He

founded the Royal Conservatory of Music, which was responsible for the preservation of most of the Han and pre-T'ang poetry that is now extant. See Note 14.

8. Orchid bloom: Should be "boneset". See Note 6.

9. Tributary flume: In the text, "the Fen River", a tributary of the Yellow River.

10. Asleep or waking: The Chinese has "rising sitting", an adverbial phrase meaning "always", "all the time".

11. Costly pin: Up to the time of the Ch'ing dynasty, Chinese women wore their hair long and done up in a coiffure.

12. The ancient bard: Refers to a stanza in the *Book of Poetry* (I, v, 10):

投我以木瓜，	Unto me a quince she threw,
報之以瓊琚，	Which with a sard I did repay—
匪報也，	No, not repay,
永以爲好也。	But prove my love for ever and aye.

(Turner's translation)

13. The happiness of a parent's spirit depends upon the remembrance of his descendants.

14. This and the following poem are songs from the Han dynasty "Royal Conservatory" collection of popular songs, which was made by order of the Emperor Wu Ti. "Royal Conservatory", the generic epithet given in this book to the collection from which these two poems are taken, is an explanatory translation of the Chinese *Yüeh fu*, literally "Musical Bureau". The name originally designated an Imperial Musical Bureau established by Han Wu-ti for the purpose of collecting popular ditties and setting them to music. Brevity being the soul of Chinese style, the name of these songs, *Yüeh fu Shih* ("Musical Bureau Poems"), was shortened to *Yüeh fu*.

The poem is a dirge for royalty and persons of noble rank.

15. From the "Royal Conservatory" collection. See note 14. "Long-song Lay" is a literal translation of the title. "Long-song Lay" and "Short-song Lay" are names of genres, both dealing with the transiency of human life. "Long" and "short" do not refer to the length or shortness of the poem, but to the degree of sonority or lightness in the music to which it was sung.

16. Our brooks that eastward reach the sea: In the China of the earlier Han dynasty (not yet extended to the southern coast), all the estuarine rivers flowed eastward into the Pacific.

17. This and the following poem "Life That's Scarce a Hundred Years" are two of the Nineteen Old Poems (古詩十九首), written by unknown authors of the Han dynasty.
    In the beginning of time, the Cowherd and the Weaving-maid loved each other so well that they neglected their work and were changed into stars by the Lord of Heaven, and stationed at either side of the Milky Way in Aquila and Lyra respectively. The lovers are permitted to meet once a year, when the wings of magpies provide a bridge for them to cross.

18. Him that held a bond with fate: More literally rendered this line would read: "The Immortal Wang Tzu-ch'iao". It refers to the son of a Chou dynasty king who attained immortality after twenty years of effort and, ultimately, flew away from this world riding on the back of a crane. (*Ed.*)

19. Ts'ao Ts'ao is one of the most dynamic personalities in Chinese history. At the collapse of the Han dynasty he made a bold bid for the emperorship and succeeded in getting away with the Northern Kingdom of Wei. By his lifelong policy of "promoting talent" he secured for his kingdom the cultural supremacy of China. His character was many-sided: he was fearless and faithless, savage yet

chivalrous, a traitor yet loyal to his friends. He is to this day the favourite "villain" of the Chinese stage. His poetry is excellent, and instinct with the dogged heroism of the old rogue.

20. Ts'ao Chih was said to be able to write fairly presentable essays at the early age of ten. His fame as a poet equals that of Ts'ao Ts'ao, his father, and that of Ts'ao P'ei, his elder brother. The victim of maltreatment at the hand of his elder brother, he often composed allegorical poems about beautiful but neglected maidens for venting grievance and sorrow. He had a compassionate heart for friends and relatives and this side of his lovable nature was reflected fully in many of his famous poems. Perhaps the best known of his poems was the one demanded by Ts'ao P'ei and composed, on pain of death in case of failure, within the set time of walking seven paces. (*Ed.*)

七步詩	Seven-Pace Song
煮豆燃豆萁，	Beans in flame that bean stalks feed
豆在釜中泣。	Out from the pan cry,
本是同根生，	"Sprung from the same stalk, what need
相煎何太急。	Each the other fry?"

(*Turner's translation*)

21. T'ao Ch'ien, styled Yüan-ming, an extremely individualistic recluse whose poetry had much influence on later writers, was well known for his immense love of wine and chrysanthemums as well as for his utter disregard for official recognition and advancement.

22. The "Peach-Blossom Fount" became a part of Chinese legend and of the poet's stock-in-trade; e.g., Wang Wei's "Peach-Blossom Fount Lay" 桃源行, a close poetical paraphrase of T'ao Yüan-ming's accompanying prose preface.

23. The First Emperor: A literal translation of Shih Huang-ti, the dynastic title assumed by the first Ch'in Emperor, who unified China, built the Great Wall, discouraged philosophical speculation and established the imperial system that lasted until 1911.

24. The extravagance and military adventures of Emperor Yang Ti (580-618), the second and last effective ruler of the Sui dynasty, brought great misery upon his subjects. The poem refers to his disastrous invasion of Korea and to the gigantic royal barge which was hauled by eighty thousand men along the canal he had constructed to join the Yangtze with the Yellow River.

25. This poem was written when the author was unjustly imprisoned in 678 A.D. by a political opponent. Subsequently, after a stormy political career, he is said to have ended his days in a monastery.

26. The T'ang Emperor Hsüan Tsung (family name Li Lung-chi, commonly called Ming Huang; 685-762) was a great soldier, poet, musician and administrator. In his later years he became a voluptuary. The story of his infatuation for Yang Kuei-fei is told in "The Song of Enduring Woe"(see pp. 168ff). In 756 A.D. he abdicated the throne in favour of his son.

27. Meng Hao-jan lived most of his life as a recluse, studying and versifying on Mount Deer-Gate, and never setting foot in the capital until the age of forty. A famous poet, he was at his best when writing on scenic beauty in the pentasyllabic form. He was a good friend of another famous nature poet, Wang Wei. (*Ed.*)

28. Wang Wei, nature poet, painter and calligraphist, who early retired from civil life to devote himself to poetry and Buddhist contemplation.

29. Li Po, most spontaneous and most charmingly egotistic of poets, was born in Szechwan of imperial stock. In youth he

was an expert swordsman, and was a wanderer and roysterer all his life. High in favour with the Emperor Ming Huang, he was banished from Court through the enmity of Imperial Consort Yang Kuei-fei, and was later under a political cloud when involved in a dynastic quarrel. In addition to the themes of wine and women, his fascination for the moon is a recurring topic. There seems no reason to disbelieve the story that he died by drowning, as he leaned intoxicated from a pleasure barge to embrace the moon's reflexion on the waters. Li Po was an ardent believer in Taoism. In reading his poetry one feels that in natural temperament, too, he is a complete Taoist, ever haunted by the beauty and magic, the mystery and pathos of existence.

30. On the stanzaic form of this translation see Preface, page 6.

31. Backward I looked . . . glimmered eerily: Literally, "Backward looking along the way I came, / Pale pale (azure-green light as of the empyrean) barred the 'Iridescent Fringe' ". 翠微 "Iridescent Fringe" is a poetical epithet for the fresh green crest of a mountain, near the summit.

32. Lines 5 and 6 and lines 7 and 8 are transposed in translation, purely for the sake of euphony.

33. Green limp tendrils at our cloaks did catch: This attempts to render 青蘿拂行衣, literally, "Deep-green limp trailing mountain vines brush against one's travelling clothes". This whole poem, in fact, is a sort of miniature "Moonlight Sonata" in verse. There are five words denoting different hues of green; and of seventy words, twenty-nine end in a vowel and nineteen in the muted -ng sound (a sound preserved better in the Cantonese dialect than in modern Mandarin pronunciation). In translating this poem, and other poems of Li Po, one can only hope to give a faint hint of the strange charm, at once earthly and unearthly, of the original.

34. The Wind . . . the Galaxy: Literally, "The song being done, the stars of the Milky Way were sparse". This has many different interpretations.

35. Merry were you . . . was I: Literally, "Drunken was I; nor sir, were you less gay".

36. Bride of Mystic Hill: Refers to the vision of a fairy maid, moving on the clouds of dawn and evening rain; seen and loved in olden times by Hsiang, the lord of the Ch'u Kingdom, upon "Wizard Hill" in Szechwan. (The hill is so named from its resemblance in shape to the Chinese ideograph meaning Wizard, 巫).

37. Flying Swallow: This was the pet name for a Han beauty who was reputedly so petite she could dance on the palm of the Emperor's hand. On the other hand, Yang Kuei-fei was considerably more fleshy; however, during the T'ang period, plumpness was considered a mark of female beauty. (*Ed.*)

38. This must be the most popular of all Chinese poems, yet many miss the point of it. It was written when the poet was exiled in South China, where frost is rarely seen. It is the semblance of frost rather than the moon that reminds him of his Northern home.

39. Ch'in Ch'uan: A place in Szechwan province which was particularly famous, during the Ch'in dynasty, for its silk handicraft.

40. Tu Fu, most illustrious of Chinese poets, was born in Shensi of Hupeh parentage. Disappointed in the public examinations, he was favoured by the Emperor Ming Huang for the excellence of his poetry. He suffered much during the rebellion of An Lu-shan and most of his life was spent in poverty and wandering. His poetry shows forth the simplicity, kindliness and great-heartedness of the man, as well as the consummate art of the poet.

41. The Great Mount is T'ai Shan (in Shantung), one of the

five sacred mountains of China. See Introduction, p.20.

42. Two lands: The names of the "two lands", 齊 and 魯, ancient principalities in Shantung, are given in the original. These monosyllables, *Ch'i* and *Lu*, would be ludicrous as well as meaningless in English verse.

43. Nature: "The Creator" could be said instead of "Nature". But in fact the Chinese phrase usually connotes the capriciousness rather than the benevolence that is seen in the world's working, and often is simply equivalent to the Greek τύχη, Chance, Luck, (Dame) Fortune.

44. Fuse and blend: Correspond to a single Chinese word, "bell" —"fuses and blends as it were metal to construct a bell".

45. Mystic beauty: Stands for "spirit(ual) splendour".

46. Literally, "Dark (female principle, of gloom and passivity) and Light (male principle, of clarity and activity) do *cut* (i.e., divide) the evening-twilight and the dawn". But a line which divides opposites can also be said to unite them; and in English, "unite", though it makes the translation less forceful than the Chinese, is more natural. The mountain is wonderfully described, so vast that one side is always sunlit, the other ever in shade.

47. From clouds upsprung: Literally, "Cleanse bosom grow (or produce) layer cloud". Layers of cloud do not normally rise from mountains: they lie on them; whereas vast mountains can be said to upspring from layers of cloud.

48. Stars alternate: Two constellations which rise and set in opposite quarters of the sky. The original gives the names of two stars that never appear in the same firmament, Ts'an (參) and Shang (商). They have a legend attached to them, about a pair of irreconcilable brothers who were banished thither.

49. Second stanza: Literally, "How long a time may youth last? The side-locks of both of us are silvered now. Enquiring about old acquaintances, half of them are become ghosts:

One cries in alarm from (or with) heated inmost bowels."
"Are become ghosts": this expression could be kept unchanged in a formal translation; but "ghost" in the sense of "one dead and gone" is so frequent in Chinese that the translation given is more exact.

50. In Autumn, 756, Tu Fu was captured by marauding forces of An Lu-shan; he thinks of his wife and children far away.

51. In yonder town: In the text the name of the town, 鄜, Fu, is given.

52. "Winsome Bride" could be rendered "fair one", "fair lady", "pretty woman", etc.; but on reading the poem through, the reader will perhaps agree that "Winsome Bride" is more appropriate.

53. Border fray: This refers to the revolt of An Lu-shan, foster son and reputed paramour of Yang Kuei-fei, in 755.

54. Titles great and proud estate: This is not a verbose rendering of 官高; the literal expression, "Height of mandarinship", did mean in Imperial China "titles great and proud estate".

55. Sweet as a lily or a rose: Literally, "Fair as jade", but this does not sound right in English. See Introduction, p.15.

56. The flower: Literally, "Shut-at-eve"; specifically it is the *Magnolia pumila*.

57. The teal: These are the pretty "Chinese teal", the "mandarin duck and drake", emblematic of wedded love and constancy.

58. Yet, all . . . love's woe: Literally, "All eyes for his new love's smiles,—what ears has he for his old love's weeping?"

59. The cypress: A symbol of fidelity in love. (Commentators remind us that the bamboos, in the next to last line, are a symbol of gentleness and honour; in the context of this particular poem, however, they need not symbolize anything.)

60. Penurious throughout his life, the poet Meng Chiao met with little success in official examinations, only managing

to pass the third degree examination at the age of fifty when most successful candidates would have been in their late teens or early twenties. The offices he held thereafter were mostly insignificant. Little wonder that in his poems the recurrent theme was one of poverty, ill luck and resentment against fate. His poetry often contains unusual phrases and expressions which attempt to convey bizarre ideas of extraordinary originality. On reading his poems one is almost certain to become imbued with a sense of melancholy and sadness. (*Ed.*)

61. O never ... her tears: Lines 9 and 10 are a very free translation of the last two lines in Chinese which, literally translated, read: "Who will say that an inch-long grass heart" (i.e., the most exiguous and ardent affection) "can requite the three-months-of-springtime radiance" (the tender and benign influence of a parent's love)? The Chinese metaphors are stock metaphors which are readily comprehensible in Chinese; but it seems impossible to reproduce them in English in such a way as to retain their force. Accordingly, I have expanded the two lines into four, first giving the meaning of the Chinese (lines 9-10), then adding two metaphors, which though somewhat different from the original, attempt to reproduce its force (lines 11-12).

62. Strange though it may seem, this delicate poem was originally intended as an allegory. The author was rejecting the overtures of a political intriguer.

63. As far as prose writing was concerned, Han Yü was the most prominent literary figure in the T'ang dynasty. It was he who began the movement against the pre-T'ang emphasis on artificial compositions of ornate and antithetical prose. He advocated a clear, simple and vigorous prose style modelled on the ancient classics. He also insisted that all prose, whatever its subject-matter, would ideally be charged with a didactic and moral tone in conformity with Confucian

teachings. He was equally well known for his poems, especially those in the 古體 ancient style, in which rare words, cacophanous phrases and difficult rhymes were purposely employed. (*Ed.*)

64. After repeated failures in the official examinations and much impoverished, Chia Tao became a monk and addressed himself seriously to the study and composition of poetry. He despised the facile and vulgar in poetry and cultivated a refined and lofty style. He was persuaded to return to secular life when a turn of luck enabled him to pass the third degree examination. He remained poor throughout his life, however, a lute and a diseased donkey being his only legacy when he died. (*Ed.*)

65. Li Ho was of royal blood and began to write poetry in his seventh year. His poetic style was bizarre and quite out of the ordinary, savouring very much of the ghostly world; hence his nick-name, "Poet-Ghost". Each morning he would go out on a horse, followed by a boy carrying a bag on his shoulder. Whenever inspired, he would immediately jot down a few lines at random, to be thrown into the bag. Back home at night, he would sort out what he had written and try to compose complete poems. This practice infuriated his mother who thought his health might be unduly undermined. This turned out to be prophetic for Li Ho died at the age of twenty-seven. (*Ed.*)

66. Phoenix Trees: This tree, which is a favourite of Chinese poets, is more beautiful than the plane-tree, with tall noble stem and great dark leaves glaucous underneath, and a profusion of flowers whiter than hawthorn in springtime See Introduction, p.22.

67. Po Chü-i, one of the greatest geniuses of China, was an earnest moralist, who on his own avowal wrote "not for the sake of letters, but for lord and liege, for people, and things and affairs". His poetry has been immensely popular

from his own day to the present: his lighter works being more admired than his serious ones. It is recorded of him that he read his poems to an illiterate old crone before publishing, that every word might be intelligible.

68. The poem "Outlandish Music" is a bit of straight talk to an Emperor. A monarch should not amuse himself with novelties: he should give all his thought to the welfare of his people.

69. This very popular narrative poem tells of the tragic infatuation of the T'ang Emperor Hsüan Tsung, the able and accomplished monarch who by his patronage of the arts was mainly responsible for the unparalleled burst of song which is the glory of T'ang times. He is said to have wandered in vision to the Palace of the Moon, where he listened to heavenly music which afterwards he transcribed under the title "Rainbow Robes and Coats of Gossamer (or Swan's down)" recurring as a sort of refrain in the poem. In middle age, he lost his heart and intelligence to the ravishingly beautiful Yang Kuei-fei, by whose creatures the government of the country was brought to ruin. In 755, An Lu-shan, the foster son of Yang Kuei-fei, marched against the Capital. The Emperor fled to Szechwan with his adored Kuei-fei. On the way he allowed her to be put to death by his generals. As the poet was treating of almost contemporaneous events, he discreetly refers to the Emperor as a "prince of Han", not a "prince of T'ang", a frequent practice by T'ang poets. He appropriately lodges the shade of Yang Kuei-fei in a Taoist Elysium; for she was a Taoist. The poem, though at first blush it may not seem so, is moral and satirical.

Wang Kuo-wei 王國維 , a famous twentieth-century critic, has commented: "This poem, despite its unusual length, is remarkable for its simplicity and originality containing only one classical allusion." (*Ed.*)

70. Eleven miles: This phrase might more accurately be rendered, "Eleven leagues". (*Ed.*)

71. Blosmy: A deliberately archaic use of "blossomy". (*Ed.*)

72. Tall forest trees: The Wu-t'ung or Phoenix tree (see Note 66). (*Ed.*)

73. South River Land is a coinage (on the analogy of Northumberland, Westmoreland, etc.) for the ugly transliteration Chiang-nan, which means "South of the (Yangtze) River" (before it changed its course in 1870). The name designated the inland area east and south of modern Shanghai proverbially renowned for the beauty of its scenery and the handsomeness of its inhabitants.

74. Wen T'ing-yün and Wei Chuang (see p. 192 and p. 194) popularized the *Tz'u* (Irregular Verse) and placed it on equal standing with the traditional forms of poetry. The style of most of the *Tz'u* writers of the early Sung dynasty was influenced by these two poets.

75. See note on previous poem (p. 193). (*Ed.*)

76. Day-dreaming: Chuang Tzu, the philosopher of the fourth century B.C., who dreamed he was a butterfly (or was it *vice versa?*).

77. The king...a bird: A legendary King of Shu (i.e., Szechwan), smitten with a hopeless passion and changed into a barbet, the Chinese counterpart of Philomel; the barbet sings at night with a harsh wailing cry—resembling the Chinese sounds for "why do you not return home"; the enchanted king weeps tears of blood from which spring the "barbet-flower", i.e., the wild azalea.

78. Tears...streaming: Mermen and mermaids rising from the sea and weeping tears of pearl—the Chinese fancy having apparently originated, like the European, in glimpses of the dugong.

79. Jade...Sward: The mists arising from Sapphire Fields (where precious stones were found) near Ch'ang-an, which

candied into jade by sunlight, and symbolized the evanescent bloom of youth.

80. An old legend tells how Ch'ang O, now the Lady of the Moon, stole the elixir of immortality which her husband had compounded. She became immortal, but was imprisoned in the moon forever.

81. Li Yü or Li Hou Chu, the last king of Southern T'ang, surrendered to the Sung and died in captivity. His *Tz'u* poems are beloved by students of Chinese literature and it is said that a *Tz'u* poem lamenting his lost kingdom was what provoked the imperial order to have him poisoned. He bewailed his harsh fate and mourned for the past life of comfort and luxury lost to him forever. His plainly descriptive style, relying solely on the strength of emotion displayed in order to impress, has much to recommend it. His best poems were written during his captivity; they are all sad and strongly pathetic, sometimes even mawkish. (*Ed.*)

82. See, the wild ... is dumb: "But voice, but word," is a literal translation of the original. These two words, put together, have only one meaning in Chinese, i.e., "news". Line 7 and line 8 together convey the idea that no news comes with the geese, conventional symbols for messengers.

83. Yen Shu was a Prime Minister of the early Sung dynasty. At the age of thirteen he had attained the second highest academic degree in the Empire. In both *Shih* and *Tz'u* forms, the grace and dignity of his style matched his official position. Even in many of his *Tz'u* where the main theme was one of sorrow, whether occasioned by parting or love lost, there was never that sense of uncontrolled despair and bitterness which characterized many a lesser poet. His love of truth and practice of frugality, self-imposed as a discipline rather than from necessity, were the distinctive qualities in his character that endeared him to the Emperor. (*Ed.*)

84. Ou-yang Hsiu was one of the greatest prose writers of his time and one who excelled as well in several varieties of polished poetry (both in traditional and *Tz'u* forms). The works of Li Po, Tu Fu and Han Yü of the T'ang dynasty seemed to have exerted a great influence over his poetic style, while his *Tz'u* all had a Five-Dynasty flavour (see Note 74). (*Ed.*)

85. Su Shih, commonly called Su Tung-p'o, was a versatile genius, stateman, *prosateur*, a first-class calligrapher, a renowned painter of bamboos and a distinguished poet. Although he writes from a Confucian background, in many of his *Shih* poems, the influence of Buddhist thoughts and Taoist ideas were clearly discernible. He enjoyed writing in the old-styled heptasyllabic form, where he could take full advantage of the freedom of space allowed to air his opinions. He excelled in the *Tz'u* form, going beyond the usual themes of romance and sorrow (especially on parting) into almost any subject—lyrical, descriptive or philosophical. It was also he who initiated the rough and free-moving style which Hsin Ch'i-chi (see Note 94), about three quarters of a century later, was to bring to perfection. Kind and compassionate, Su Shih thrived on friendship, having an implicit faith in the innate goodness of human nature. It was particularly ironical that many of his closest friends betrayed him, even to the extent of soliciting his death, just because of a difference in political opinions. Su Shih's deep-rooted dislike for Wang An-shih's new reform policy was the main cause of his vicissitudes and of a life spent mostly in banishment. (*Ed.*)

86. The Western Lake is compared to Hsi Shih, "the Western Maid", a beauty of ancient times, whose occasional frown enhanced her charms.

87. Written after the Juchen Tartar invasion in 1125, when the writer's husband, Chao Ming-ch'eng, was dead. The first

eight lines attempt to communicate something of the
Chinese reduplicative *tour de force*:

> *Hsün hsün mi mi,*
> *Leng leng ch'ing ch'ing,*
> *Ch'i ch'i ts'an ts'an ch'i ch'i.*

The "pine and peak" of the first line is reminiscent of
Shakespeare's "peak and pine", meaning to "waste away".
(*Ed.*)

88. Broad leaves: Refers to the Wu-t'ung tree. See Note 66 and
Introduction, p.22 (*Ed.*)

89. Written after Chao Chi had been dethroned and led into
exile by the Juchen Tartars.

90. "Wide lakes . . . plains of dust": These words are not in the
original. They are added to carry over some of the force of
the original Chinese in the preceding line, "And such a
world of distance lies between".

91. The translator has deliberately changed the original "sixth-
month" references (based on the Chinese lunar calendar
system) to the "seventh-month", since June is a relatively
mild month while July more effectively communicates the
hot summer atmosphere desired here. (*Ed.*)

92. Lu Yu, one of the best known poets of the Southern Sung
dynasty, was undoubtedly among the most patriotic poets
in the history of Chinese literature (see Introduction, page
11). There were many facets to the colourful life he lived
but before he died at the grand old age of eighty-six, he was
to look upon his past with mixed feelings of regret and
resentment: regret because protracted border wars made
it impossible to unite the empire (see p. 271); resentment,
because the last twenty years of his life were spent in
unwilling retirement. He claims to have composed "ten
thousand poems in the space of sixty years". As a matter of
fact, we have now more than nine thousand poems preserved

and, despite claims of repetitiousness, many of them are really of the very first order. Later critics were unanimous in their praise of the many heptasyllabic Regulated Verses that came from his pen. (*Ed.*)

93. Sacred rite: Refers to the customary worship rendered by a son to the spirit of his dead parent.

94. Hsin Ch'i-chi was the most patriotic writer in Irregular Verse, saying what he felt in a straightforward manner. He was well-versed in the classics and so literary allusions abound in his poems, but without any design to ostentatiously parade his learning. Two periods of enforced retirement in middle age enabled him to produce many of his best-known poems where love of nature or a sense of frustration over inactivity was the recurrent theme. He actually fought many a battle in his early twenties and in his old age when he talked about the war and his futile desire to join the army again for active service, it was not an empty boast or some flight of poetic fancy. His name is often linked with Su Shih (see Note 85) and the term "Su-Hsin" has come to denote free-moving and rough style in *Tz'u* writing which later poets would admire but could never adequately imitate. (*Ed.*)

95. Wen T'ien-hsiang was a prime minister under the last effectively reigning Sung emperor. He was imprisoned by the Mongols while negotiating a truce with them. He escaped and raised an army to make a last desperate stand against the now established invaders. In 1280 he was defeated in Kwangtung by the irresistible forces of Kublai Khan and led into captivity to Cambaluc, by the site of modern Peking. After three years' imprisonment, during which the Mongols made every effort to win him to their allegiance, he was beheaded. (*Ed.*)

96. The Tomb Feast Eve, in Chinese 寒食 "Chill Eve" (on which day by ancient prescription, in commemoration of a

retired minister accidentally burned alive, no fires were lit),
is the day preceding 清明, the "Clear-Bright", the Festival
of the Tomb. On this day in April (about Eastertime)
Chinese families go up *en masse* to their ancestral tombs—
with a reverence and filial devotion which is truly touching
—to mourn their dead, clean (or, as they say, "sweep") the
tombs, burn incense and paper money and offer their
sacrifices of rice and wine.

97. Years of war: Refers to the struggles that preceded the
setting up of the Ming dynasty. The author, a famous
"archaizing" writer, having offended the first Ming emperor
by a composition of his, was publicly hacked in two!

98. Ancient glories . . . lived in ancient days: See Introduction,
p.21.

99. Since . . . vapour: To compensate for the relative vague-
ness of the first stanza, the translation of the second is
made more "snappy" than the author's.

100. Yet, mark . . . you'll find: Literally, "Look, my friend,
at a man who is in the realm of drunkenness, / You'll find
he is in the 'opening of Heaven and Earth' ".

101. "Yüan-ming" refers to the famous poet T'ao Yüan-ming
whose love for wine was proverbial. See Note 21. (*Ed.*)

102. This is a poem celebrating a victory against Japanese pirates.

103. Lips sealed tight: Soldiers wore wooden gags when silence
was required.

104. Nalan, a Manchurian, was the son of the prime minister
Ming Chu. After passing the third degree examination he
was appointed personal guard to the Emperor. He was a
well-known poet during his lifetime (especially famous for
the shorter *Tz'u* forms) and equally versed in calligraphy,
horsemanship and archery. In his official capacity as the
imperial guard, he frequently accompanied the Emperor to
remote parts of the empire like the bleak, cold North as
well as many famous mountains long held sacred. Hence

the rough and hardy airs in many of his *Tz'u* poems. His *Tz'u* style was often likened both by contemporary and later critics to that of Li Yü (see Note 81) for the depth of genuine feelings conveyed as well as for the plain and direct way in which these feelings were expressed without resorting to artificial devious literary devices. But an undertone of sadness and grief, probably born of poor health and an alleged ill-fated love affair, pervades many of his poems. He died at the age of thirty-one. (*Ed.*)

105. In a prose preface to this poem, the author relates how three days before the Double-Ninth Festival in 1677, he dreamed about his sorrowing wife who had already died. In the dream she spoke these poetic lines before parting: "In my constant woe I would fain be the moon in heaven, year by year to shine upon my beloved at the full". The author expresses surprise that she who never wrote poetry in her life should compose such touching verses. Upon awaking he wrote the long poem which follows.

Author Index

Title Index

First Line Index

340

342

The Translator

In Memoriam: Father John A. Turner, S.J.

1909-1971

Father John Turner first went to Hong Kong from Ireland in 1935, already a mature scholar of classical Gaelic, Latin and Greek. From the time of his arrival in Hong Kong, he took the study of Chinese language and literature as his main task in life. In addition to his great interest in and love for Chinese culture, he added Chinese painting and calligraphy to his artistic accomplishments. From 1947 to 1949, he was professor of European Literature at Sun Yat-sen National University, Canton. Apart from two periods in Ireland and about a year in Taiwan, the last thirty-six years of his life were spent in Hong Kong teaching English Literature and Translation as well as working on an English-Cantonese dictionary. One of his particular interests was spoken Cantonese in its various styles and unwritten expressions, popular speech and drama. The use, and abuse, of language was a subject of endless fascination and discussion for him.

A charming and handsome man, highly cultured, his varied talents and literary abilities, however, did suffer from lack of discipline, and he published very little, and that little mostly in journals. He was a perfectionist, and for many years worked on his translations, testing them out on various friends, changing a word here and there, adding to the collection. To a prospective publisher, he wrote quite candidly: "You may be surprised at the speed with which I turn out translations; but I assure you they are not 'rushed.' I have read and made notes on well over 2000 poems while selecting them. And very often I will have a poem all but translated except for a *mot juste* or a grammatical difficulty. Many of the poems I have shown you are an instance of what might be called 'delayed subconscious activity'."

Notwithstanding Father Turner's meticulous scholarship (e.g. paging through Chinese books on botany to track down the accurate name for an unusual flower) and serious dedication (e.g. rereading all of Spenser in order to get himself in the mood to reproduce a certain archaic poetical flavor to a translation), his success is better represented by the sensitive outpouring of the heart of an artist in love with the Chinese people and their literary language. He valued the good opinion of the few whose judgement he respected, but he had little interest in public fame and seemed to believe that all that really mattered was to do first-class work and communicate it to the few in his intellectual and literary circle that could appreciate it.

His strong, independent character was usually colored with good humor and gentleness, and his frustrations and annoyance not infrequently issued in verse or limericks which were amusing and never bitter or hurtful. On one occasion, when some of his translations were accused of being sentimental, he said: "Sentimentality is a Germanic virtue. And the tincture of guileless Cromwellian blood in my own veins has long been overlaid with the serum of Celtic cynicism. The most sentimental lines I ever wrote were these (on an attack of indigestion diagnosed as *angina*):

> If, as they say, I have no heart—alack,
> How should I suffer from a heart attack.

—the point of the remark being that my friends do say it."

The sad irony of this stroke of wit is that Father Turner, after years of crippling arthritis and bad health, died of a severe heart attack on December 21, 1971.

The Editor

Fr. John J. Deeney, Ph.D., a fellow Jesuit and close friend of Fr. Turner, has been in the Far East for over 16 years. His interest in Chinese Literature began in 1956 when he began studying Mandarin in Taiwan, an interest which he has pursued ever since in his teaching of English and Comparative Literature. On a number of occasions he has returned to his native America to lecture on Chinese Literature.

When not teaching at National Taiwan University in Taipei, he is occupied with research and publication of materials related to East-West cultural exchange. He was one of the editors and translators of the recently published *Anthology of Contemporary Chinese Literature, Taiwan: 1949-1974* (Vol. 1—Poems and Essays, Vol. 2—Short Stories). His other publications include an *Annotated Bibliography of English, American and Comparative Literature for Chinese Scholars*, co-edited with Professor Chi Ch'iu-lang; *Style Manual and Transliteration Tables for Mandarin*; and a series of Study Guides for difficult works in English and American Literature, featuring annotations in Chinese, done in collaboration with his Chinese colleagues in Taipei.

His current scholarly concern lies in promoting Chinese-Western literary relations through careful re-thinking of the Theory and Methodology of Comparative Literature from a Far Eastern perspective. This is also the subject matter of a course which he teaches in the newly established doctoral program at National Taiwan University.

RENDITIONS Books

General Editors

Stephen C. Soong
George Kao